WITCHCRAFT FOR THE HOME

Witchcraft for the Home

Spells, Rituals, and Remedies for a Magical Dwelling

MYSTIC DYLAN

ROCKRIDGE PRESS

No book, including this one, can ever replace the diagnostic expertise and medical advice of a physician in providing information about your health. The information contained herein is not intended to replace medical advice. You should consult with your doctor before using the information in this or any health-related book.

First Rockridge Press trade paperback edition 2022

For general information on our other products and services, please contact our Customer Care Department within the United States at (866) 744-2665, or outside the United States at (510) 253-0500.

Paperback ISBN: 978-1-63878-167-7
Hardcover ISBN: 979-8-88608-646-1
eBook ISBN: 978-1-63807-766-4

Manufactured in the United States of America

Interior and Cover Designer: Michael Cook
Art Producer: Melissa Malinowsky
Editor: Carolyn Abate
Production Editor: Ellina Litmanovich
Production Manager: Holly Haydash

Title Page: Illustrations by Mary Woodin
Illustration © 2022 Mary Woodin; Author photo courtesy of Olivia Graves

10 9 8 7 6 5 4 3 2 1 0

This book is dedicated to those new to the path of witchcraft and to those who came before us. To my parents, my grandmother, and my fierce friends and mentors who've supported and encouraged me.

CONTENTS

PART I

An Introduction to Witchcraft for the Home

Here in your hands, you hold a sacred tome, a magical text that will help you transform your humble living quarters into a divine temple. Within these pages, you'll discover not only how to strengthen a magical bond with your home, but also how to access its powers, and work with the spirits, ancestors, and magical allies that surround your household. Whether in the kitchen, living room, or bedroom, even the smallest of spaces can provide a wondrous environment for house witchery. As you move through book be sure to use the notes section in the back to keep track of your experiences.

CHAPTER 1

Magic and the Homestead

A witch honors all that is sacred: from natural wonders, such as caves and hot springs, to ancient monuments, such as the pyramids of Giza or the Oracle of Delphi, and countless other examples. But what is sacred above all else for the witch is the home. It is your temple, your laboratory, and your sanctuary. In this chapter, we begin by exploring what exactly witchcraft for the home is and what it looks like in practice. We also dive in and explore the history of the witch's home. Finally, you'll learn about the sacred power of the hearth and its central place in house witchery.

So, what is witchcraft for the home?

Witchcraft for the home, or "house witchery," as I like to call it, is the use of sorcery centered around the household. House witchery consists of spells, rituals, charms, and remedies that protect, cleanse, and work with the spirits of the household.

Witchcraft for the home is predominantly centered around protection, as well as connecting with ancestors and household spirits. The witch and their home have a sacred bond so powerful that the imagery has been forever immortalized in folklore and fairy tales. Take, for instance, the witch with her house made of sweets in the German tale of "Hansel and Gretel," or Baba Yaga, the supernatural enchantress from Slavic legend, who resides in a chicken-legged hut. These tales also show that the witch's home is far from mundane, but rather it is an enchanted fortress. The home of the witch is magical in itself, as the spirit of the home is awakened by the witch who resides within it. The home offers the witch protection as well as a space in which to make magic. Think of house witchery as not only doing magic for the home, but also using the energy and magic of the home.

THE HISTORY OF WITCHCRAFT IN THE HOME

Witchcraft in the home can be traced back to when humankind first sought shelter in caves. One of the first-known magical illustrations is in the Trois Frères cave in France. Dating back to 13,000 BCE, one of these cave paintings depicts a man shape-shifting into a stag. The discovery not only links the practice of magic to the household, but also solidifies that the practice of magic is Paleolithic in age.

As societies evolved, so did the practice of magic. With the building of villages and cities came the arrival of temples and sacred structures for prayer and the worship of deities. However, for many common folk, a small altar or sacred space was designated in the home to honor local deities, household spirits, and ancestors.

Throughout history, witches have performed their magic in the household. Since the dawn of most structured religions, much of spiritual services are taught and sought in a church or temple. However, the witch does not need to visit a temple or be part of any religious organization to perform their magic. They practice from the confines of their home, often acting in secret to avoid speculation, persecution, and scrutiny.

Modern Home Witchcraft

The practice of house witchery has changed drastically since the days of yore. The home was a shelter and sanctuary for many who practiced their craft in secret. Today, witches need not hide behind closed doors. The home has transformed from a shelter to a temple, where every facet of the home can serve magical purposes. The tenets for house witchery remain pretty much unchanged:

- Claim your space and make it your home.
- Cleanse and protect frequently.
- Honor your ancestors and house spirits.
- Create altars for magic and ritual.

Other Forms of Home Magic

Before we explore house witchery, we must first establish one thing: Witchcraft is a practice that is not restricted by labels. Practicing house magic does not confine you to refer to yourself as a house witch. Performing witchcraft for the home encompasses many other forms of witchery and magic, such as kitchen witchery, green witchery, and workings for protection and cleansing. By performing witchcraft for the home, you'll discover other forms of magic, such as bindings, crafting amulets and talismans, divination, and even necromancy. Think of your home as the cauldron and all the different forms of magic and witchery as the ingredients to help strengthen your craft.

EVERY HOME IS A MAGICAL HOME

A home is a place where a person or family lives, and while I may use the word "house" from time to time, I am not referring to a specific structure, but rather to a building where one lives, either alone or with family, friends, or housemates. The term "house" can also refer to a place for those seeking shelter, a facility that cares for animals, or a residence for a spiritual or educational community.

Homes come in a variety of sizes, and living situations are different for everyone. If your living quarters feel like home, that's all that matters. Regardless of whether you rent or own or you are living with family, by yourself, or with roommates, if you feel connected to the space, then it's a home and it's ready for you to make magic in it.

It's also important to remember that the architecture, design, and construction of your space does not dictate whether you're a witch and your home is magical. Many people get caught up in the aesthetics of what they feel witchcraft should *look* like. You don't have to live in an abandoned castle with antique gargoyle sconces or a cottage deep in the woods to be a witch or practice witchcraft.

Sacred at Any Square Footage

The size of your home does not dictate the size of your power or magic. Whether you live in a studio apartment in the city, a grand manor in the country, or your childhood bedroom, your home is magical and should be treated as such. The success of your spells, rituals, and magical workings will not be affected by the size of your space, but by the energy and dedication you put into the magic that you're doing and how you treat the space you're in. If you are disconnected from your home and don't feel comfortable in it, you'll have a challenging time working your magic effectively, regardless of the size of the space. You must feel comfortable in your space and make it your own.

Sacred in Any Region

Witchcraft is bioregional, meaning that the type of magic you do and the spirits with which you work will vary depending on where you're from and where you're living. Home magic is a way to honor "the spirit of place." The folklore, herbs, stones, and animals are all different wherever you go. You must acknowledge the sacred sites, flora, and fauna of where you live in order to have a deeper connection to your home and its surrounding geography. Magic has been practiced for millennia by every civilization in every part of the world. I guarantee there's a trace of lore and magic where you're living right now; it's up to you to uncover its history and tap into its power.

Honoring Personal Histories and Memories

We all have had different life experiences and living situations. Some of us grew up in one household for our entire childhood, while others have moved a lot or traveled around the globe. Throughout our lives, we develop connections to the spaces we've called home, our surroundings, and the faces that come with those surroundings.

These interactions and exchanges of energy create the bond we have to a specific space, thus leaving residual energy, even after we're gone. History is an important facet of house witchery, and not just the history of the space when you arrive, but the history you make when you're there. The dining room in which your family used to gather for holiday dinners or birthday celebrations, the kitchen where you helped your grandmother bake, or the bedroom in which you slept as a child holds energy that permeates into the space. When I visit my grandmother's home in Miami, I am often flooded with memories and have felt the presence of my dogs and cat from childhood lingering—even though they have passed.

To have successful results in spellwork for your home, you must first feel that your living space *is* a home. Good memories, comfortable spaces, and an environment reflective of your personality all help create a homey space.

THE MAGIC OF THE HEARTH

It all began with fire, the first true magic. Think of the first flame as the spark of creation. Fire was the gateway to all magic, for it was around a fire that humans huddled together for warmth and shared stories about the cosmos, formed our vast mythologies, named the spirits we honor and work with, and forged our craft. Around the fire, we danced for a bountiful harvest, cooked our meals, and burned our sacrifices in hopes of appeasing the divine. Eventually, our fire was contained and given proper recognition in our homes, as the beginnings of the sacred hearth.

When we think of the word "hearth" today, we may instinctively think of a fireplace. However, the hearth was much more than that. It was the gathering place, reminiscent of the bonfire around which people would huddle. The hearth was often seen as a space for warmth and protection. The hearth was so central to home life in ancient times and civilizations that it became sacred. Many deities around the world are connected to the hearth and its sacred flame, which we will explore in depth later.

In ancient Rome, the goddess Vesta was connected to the hearth—so much so that a perpetual flame had to be kept lit in her honor in her sacred temple and guarded at all hours by her priestesses, known as the vestal virgins.

Even in private homes, ancient Romans set up altars around the hearth and honored the sacred goddess.

For witches, the hearth has always been extremely important, as it is also known as a liminal space, standing between this world and the next. The hearth was deemed a portal through which one could communicate with and travel to the other side.

The hearth was not just a gateway to the spirits of the deceased but to those of the supernatural realm as well. Faeries, elves, and other creatures were known to enter homes via the hearth. Even in modern times, the hearth is still considered a portal. Take for example the tale of Santa Claus, who travels up and down a chimney to disperse gifts.

Architecture has changed over time, and the hearth is not as central to modern homes as it once was. Fortunately, it is not necessary to have a hearth, and if you don't have one, this will not affect your magical practice. Today, the hearth is replaced by many modern witches, pagans, and magical practitioners with a dedicated space for an altar and the use of candles to represent the sacred flame. This way, the hearth lives on as a mindset and transforms from fireplace to sacred space.

HOW THE HOME CAN ENHANCE YOUR MAGIC WORK

The home is a vital asset to the witch. Not only does it provide shelter, but it also becomes a sacred space. First, we must look at the main thing a house provides: protection. Within the confines of your home, you can safely perform your spells and rituals. While one could easily go to a random clearing to do spellwork, being in your home allows you the privacy and time to truly commit to your spellcraft. At home, you have access to all your tools without having to plan ahead and make sure you pack everything you need. Once you establish that your home is your sacred space, the spirits and energies residing within the space will work with you and further enhance your magical workings.

Don't get me wrong, I absolutely love doing rituals in nature or outside. Witches throughout history performed magic in the woods, by rivers, on beaches, and even in cemeteries. Still, there's nothing more profound than being able to let loose in the privacy of your own space.

Establishing a Spiritual Space

The witch's home is a temple, a sacred space for magic and ritual, and a conduit to the spirit realm. As witches, we should treat our homes as such. This does not mean that you need to deck out your entire space with crystals, skulls, and spiritual memorabilia, but you should at least have one spot in your home where your magical tools and books can reside. Establishing a spiritual space also requires cleansing the home of any unhelpful energies. This can be done through spiritual fumigation, the burning of sacred herbs or incense, or by using spiritual waters, such as Florida water, holy water, or rue water, which we will discuss in a later chapter.

Supporting Those Who Dwell There

If you don't live alone, then you'll also have to incorporate those who reside within your dwelling into your spiritual space. This doesn't mean they need to share your beliefs, or even be aware of your practice, but it does mean that you need to establish a sense of protection both for them and from them. Perhaps you have a roommate who does not share your values around witchcraft; you can still do a protection spell for the home, but be considerate about how and when you decide to perform the spell or ritual. You always want to be mindful of those with whom you share space. Placing protective crystals around the house can be just as effective as a full-on smoke cleansing session, which may affect someone's allergies or simply spook some people.

Enhancing a Witch's Magical Path

Before we pull out the cauldron and start conjuring up spells and spirits, we must first establish our practice and have a keen sense of our path and how we'd like to follow it. Why are you attracted to witchcraft? Why do you want to cast a spell? What kind of magic are you looking to practice? All these are necessary questions you should ask yourself before you start throwing herbs in a pot, lighting candles, and hoping for the best. The witch always knows their why! They understand the magical properties of herbs and why they're used in certain spells. They understand the folklore and mythology surrounding certain deities and spirits. They are familiar with the sacred tools they are using and understand their origins and magical properties. Remember, knowledge is power. You will need to know the history and folklore surrounding certain tools, flora, and fauna to establish a coherent and safe practice. Read as much as you can, and start your occult/magical library. Explore different aspects of witchcraft—maybe look at folk magic that is tied to your ancestry and genealogical roots. You may be amazed at what you find.

Nurturing a Witch's Power

We all need to recharge from time to time, and that is especially true for the witch, who is constantly using the energies around them. A witch must have a space of their own in which to decompress and relax. For the witch to nurture their power, they must feel safe and secluded. This is why privacy is so important. Find a space to call your own where you can escape from the outside world. Add a comfy blanket, some calming music, a favorite crystal, and anything else that helps you relax. Selenite, a salt-based crystal, is perfect for cleansing and renewing magical energy. Carrying black stones such as hematite, tourmaline, and onyx is also great for protection and grounding.

CREATING AND MAINTAINING A SANCTUARY

To create your sanctuary, you must first claim your space by purging it of any negative or unwelcome energies and establishing an energetic connection to the space. Connecting to your space and building a relationship with it is vital to performing magic successfully. To transform your home into a sanctuary, you must first fill the newly cleansed space with positive vibrations. Play some music that makes you happy and let yourself dance and twirl around your space as you wish. Brush your hands along the walls and envision blue light flowing from your fingertips and painting the walls with your positive energy. Since you are the witch, it is your task to create your sacred space.

Think of things that bring you joy as you walk around your home, and touch items to imbue them with your energy. Take a few crystals, hold them in your hands, close your eyes, and envision them being charged with magical energy. Hide them throughout the house to enchant your space and enhance your magic.

Shaping Energy

Witchcraft is the manipulation of energy. We use energy and magic to shape the world around us. While it may sound difficult, it really isn't. The key to shaping energy is visualization and belief. The witch must believe that they can shape and alter energy for it to be so. I like to visualize energy as a beam of colored light emitting from my hands.

Close your eyes, take a few deep breaths, and envision this ball of light emanating from your palms. Put all your positive thoughts and intentions into that ball of energy and then send it out, directing it through your space, touching objects you wish to give that energy to. Witches shape energy for various reasons, such as to cast circles of protection during spellwork, to send energy and spellwork directly into an object, and to engage in astral travel, so theirs is a talent to harness and strengthen.

Guiding Energy

Guiding energy can be accomplished in a multitude of ways, but the simplest is by using a tool that is designated specifically for directing energy, such as a crystal point, wand, ritual blade, or even your very own finger. Witches have been using wands, scepters, and daggers for ritual and for directing energy for centuries. Meditate on which tool calls to you when you wish to guide energy. If you'd simply like to use your finger, perhaps find a ring to wear that you can concentrate on and use when directing energy. If you decide to use a tool like a wand or ritual blade, make sure that you cleanse it first to remove all energies that might've attached to it. These tools can then be used to cast a circle, consecrate other objects, and direct energy in your spellwork.

Maintaining Energy

Witches can maintain a household's energy by creating an altar and working with the spirits of the home. An altar is a sacred space that is either dedicated to deities and spirits or used for magic and spellwork. You should regularly perform a ritual to cleanse the house and connect to the altar. In ancient Rome, the beginning of each month was known as the *kalends*, and it is considered a good time to perform such rituals.

THE MAGIC OF THE HOME BEGINS WITH YOU

Do you want to transform your home into a magical abode? Then do it! You have the power; now you just have to believe in yourself. The magic resides within you. Regardless of whether you've been practicing witchcraft for decades or started rather recently, you have what it takes to create powerful and effective house witchery. The path there starts by wanting to perform such magic, then believing yourself capable, doing your research, and engaging in actual practice. If you've stumbled upon this book and you're reading this, then you're ready to start.

Remember that the magic of the home resides within the home. Get acquainted with your living space: Sit on the floor in the middle of the space or in your room and close your eyes. What memories or feelings come up? What do you know about the space? What is your particular history with the space? Getting comfortable with the energy of the space is step one. Working witchcraft into your everyday life is another component to house witchery, and it's simpler than it sounds. To the witch, there is magic in everything. Making yourself a morning cup of coffee or tea? Stir in some sugar clockwise to sweeten the day. Cleaning the floors? Use Florida water or some vinegar with lemon to wash away the tracks of those you no longer wish to have come into your space.

RESPECTING COMMUNAL AND INDIVIDUAL AREAS

When transforming your home into a sacred sanctuary, first decide which areas are private, personal spaces and which are communal. Once you've designated these sections of the home, you can contemplate how best to use your magic in these areas. For example, the living room, which is the successor to the hearth, is a place for gatherings of friends and family, making this space better suited for spells and rituals dealing with ancestral veneration, attracting friendships, and maintaining a supportive community. The bedroom, however, is a more intimate and private space, well suited to performing astral projection, sex magic, love spells, and more private workings. The bathroom is used for personal cleansing and purification.

Since tools are a necessary part of the craft, think of this when doing witchcraft in communal areas. How apparent do you want your practice to be to others? Some of the most powerful tools in a witch's arsenal are common household products, which can make their use quite discreet. Take, for example, the witch's besom, or broom: Propped with the bristles up by the doorway, it protects the home from malignant spirits and negative energies. There are many potent yet discreet forms of magic for the home that will not raise the suspicions of family and friends. A horseshoe nailed above the door is another powerful totem used not only to ward off evil, but also to attract luck. Salt sprinkled along the doorways and windowsills will also offer protection. Then, of course, there's a plethora of plants that can be kept to invoke various kinds of magic.

KEY TAKEAWAYS

You've come so far! Before we delve further into the magic that is house witchery, here are a few things to remember, review, and practice.

- The magical aspects of a home and sacred space are not dependent on its size, architecture, or decor but rather on you and your connection with the space.
- House witchery is not a stand-alone practice and blends into other forms of magic, such as candle magic, kitchen magic, and spirit work.
- Enhance your magical path by researching and studying witchcraft, folk magic, and spellwork.
- Cleanse your space and connect with your environment regularly.
- Practice harnessing and directing energy, and focus on how you will use that to strengthen your connection to your home.
- Be mindful of communal areas, and figure out how these spaces will be used in your witchcraft.
- Remember that magic is everywhere, and even the most basic household items might have a magical history.
- The home is a witch's sanctuary, so use your energy and witchcraft to turn your living space into a sacred and magical space.
- Connect with the history of your home, regardless of whether you're part of it.
- Acknowledge the spirits and energies of the space.

CHAPTER 2

The Power of the House Witch

We've covered the basics, so now it's time to apply what we've learned and take a step further into the realm of house witchery. In this chapter, we will explore the benefits of practicing witchcraft in the home as well as how to properly execute your magic, spellwork, and rituals. You will learn some basic techniques and tenets, as well as other magical elements to incorporate into your house witchery practice, such as the use of elements, lunar phases, and astrology. The more you learn about house witchery, the more you'll come to realize that it's an eclectic practice.

THE BENEFITS OF USING WITCHCRAFT IN THE HOME

If you are a witch, it stands to reason that you would practice witchcraft in your own home. This is vital to you as a person *and* as a witch. When you work your magic in the home, you strengthen the bond you have with your home. Before you jump into any spell, it is essential to reinforce your connection with your space by cleansing it and grounding yourself in it. This connection transforms your home into a fortress and temple that can both protect and support you as you perform your magical workings. Think of it as siphoning energy from your home to feed your spells. If you look at the practice of animism and the belief that all things contain spirit, imagine all the energy at your disposal. Wood, rock, granite, brick, and even metal objects hold energy that can be harnessed in your craft. This is the energy you utilize to create your sacred space and establish a comfortable environment. This is the power of the house witch.

Comfort

We've established that the witch must feel comfortable in their living space to perform successful house witchery, but did you know that you can achieve this comfort by actually using witchcraft? It's true. Burning incense, meditating, performing rituals to connect to the space, and enchanting items like furniture are just a few ways to enhance the comfort of your home. When you feel content, that feeling seeps into the home, providing a comfortable energy throughout. Imagine, if you will, being synced with the house via magical Bluetooth.

Protection

When you establish a connection to your home, the two of you share a magical bond. Protection is probably the most critical element of magic that should be performed in the home. It further links your magic and energy to your space, making you stronger both magically and physically. When you perform protection magic in your home, you're protecting yourself since you reside within the home, so it's a magical combination of sorts—two for the price of one.

Sustenance

The kitchen is not only the sacred space used for conjuring up a variety of spells, but it is also used to create food used for sustenance. Kitchen witchery is an integral component of house witchery since we need nourishment to live. However, many of the foods and ingredients used in the kitchen contain magical properties that are also useful in witchcraft and house witchery. You'll be surprised by just how many items for your witchcraft you can obtain from the grocery store.

Creativity

Once you establish your home as an entity with spirit, you'll realize that it needs to be fed and that it has its own energy and sometimes personality. The personality of the home should be an extension of yourself. Witchcraft exists because people believe it exists; magic is creation. When you let yourself explore your self-expression and creativity, whether it be through art, decor, or cooking up a unique meal, you're feeding the energy of the house. Release your creativity, use it in your magic, and see how the energy in your home vibrates with positivity and reinforces your creative feelings.

Spiritual Nourishment

Reading about witchcraft is not enough. You must practice the craft as well. Often, witches can get distracted or drained by the mundane world. When you dedicate your home as a sacred space, you will constantly feel spiritually nourished. Practices like cleansing yourself and your home, maintaining an altar, and displaying and working with sacred objects can all help restore your energy and keep your home feeling spiritually connected.

THE PARTICULAR MAGIC OF THE KITCHEN

The kitchen is central not only to house witchery but also to civilization. Remember the importance of fire. In today's modern home, the kitchen is where we use fire to create meals that sustain us and those we love. As a matter of fact, the kitchen, cooking, and food are pretty essential to many religious gatherings and celebrations, as they have been for many millennia.

The kitchen has undergone drastic changes throughout history. In many early households, it was in a completely different building, or cooking took place outside in the yard. Eventually, the kitchen made its way into the home as its own designated room. This room had multiple uses, including for storage and laundry. As the twentieth century approached, we began to downsize, and the kitchen more often merged with the dining area, once again connecting us to the idea of communal cooking and feasting.

You may find that as a witch, your primary spot for performing magic is the kitchen. This is because the kitchen is the witch's laboratory, and many of the items, ingredients, and tools you'll be using for witchcraft already reside there. Pots for boiling water, cutting boards for chopping herbs, and wooden spoons to stir your concoctions are all part of house witchery.

CONNECTING WITH YOUR HOME'S ENERGY

You must establish an energetic connection to your sacred space to see successful results in your spellwork. Creating and maintaining an energetic connection to your home is not as challenging as it may seem. First, your living space must feel like a home. A good way to make your space feel homey is by adding your personal touch to your space using decor, furniture, childhood items, and collectibles. While this may seem like a mundane approach, remember that the things you love carry meaning, and thus what you cherish raises the vibration of your space.

Another simple way of connecting to your home's energy is by cleaning it. Yes, this may seem tedious, but cleaning is a large part of house witchery, and many cleaning supplies and tools have magical significance, including vinegar, lemon, brooms, and water. Once your space is clean, find your favorite spot to just sit and relax. Take a nap, let your mind wander, and absorb the energies of your home. Using divination is also a great way to connect with your space. Do a reading on your home. Whether using a pendulum, oracle cards, or tarot, ask questions about your living space and your future in it, and see what comes up. This will help further solidify the bond between you and your home's energy.

THE RELATIONSHIP BETWEEN YOUR MAGIC AND YOUR INTENTIONS

The magic you create, the spells you cast, and the energy you give off are all a direct extension of you and therefore will affect not only you but also your home. When you venture into the realm of witchcraft and start using magic and spellwork, do so with clear intention, considering the long-term effects your magic can have.

Spells are very real. There are many questions to ask yourself before casting a spell: What is it that you want? How will getting what you want affect others?

If you start using magic and doing spells on a whim, without clear intentionality, you may find yourself and others negatively affected, along with the energy in your home and sacred space. Your home is also an extension of you, so if you are irrational and stressed and start performing spells without proper care and consideration for yourself and others, your home will mirror that erratic energy. It is always best to meditate and give ample thought to your intended outcome before performing any kind of witchcraft.

Divination is another wonderful way to gain insight about whether to perform a spell. Read about the situation to see if it's worth pursuing or if a spell will make what you want more tangible. Remember that once you send out that energy, it can't be undone; it can only be changed.

FINDING MAGIC IN THE MUNDANE

Witches know that magic is all around us and that almost any object can have magical properties, regardless of how mundane it may seem. Why is there magic in the mundane? Probably because witches did not always have access to the kinds of occult items that we can easily buy today and had to make do with what they had. For example, salt is known to absorb moisture, so magically, salt absorbs negative energies and protects the perimeter of the home when sprinkled around it. Another common household item that is strongly linked to witches is the broom. Its mundane function is to sweet up dirt and dust. For witches, the broom also clears space magically and is used for protection and astral travel.

The cauldron is a large pot, usually made of cast iron, though in some ancient civilizations, it was made of bronze. The cauldron represents the sacred womb, a source of creation. This is where witches would **conjure** up magical oils, tinctures, and potions. The cauldron is a vessel within which magic can be created. Today, any cooking pot can represent the cauldron and maintain that magical connection. You see? The mundane realm is filled with magical tools that are beneficial to the house witch.

HOW YOU DEFINE "HOME" IS MEANINGFUL

The word "home" means many things to many people, and every witch will have a different idea of what a home is to them. Generally, once a witch truly feels connected to and safe within their space, the house becomes a home. A house is just living quarters, but a home provides an emotional connection, a sense of security, and an uplifting energy that you feel when you're in that space. The witch's home should be a space where they can go to recharge and escape from stress.

The home of the witch is magical in every sense of the word, so much so that those who visit the space sometimes feel it as soon as they walk in. Think about places that you've considered homey. What made them feel that way? How can you mirror that feeling in your space?

Household Members

Each witch will have a unique family that they call their own. Some families may be chosen; others may be the family you were born into. Whatever your situation, there's nothing like being able to share your magical space with others when you can. If you already live with family or friends, you'll learn that house witchery doesn't just benefit you but also the other people who reside in your household.

When friends and family visit your space, they leave behind residual energy with which the home becomes familiar the more they visit. Not only do you have an energetic connection with these individuals, but your home does as well, making spellwork you perform for these people in your home increase in effectiveness.

The more positive and happy life experiences you have within your space, the more it becomes a home and the more those positive energies will be stored within its walls. On days when you feel stressed out, tired, or just down, that energy is there to help restore you.

Home Values

We all have personal values, often adopted from or molded by our personal upbringing. What are your values? How do they affect your home and your magic? Unlike other spiritual paths, witchcraft doesn't adhere to any strict tenets.

Wicca, the religion whose practitioners refer to themselves as witches, adheres to what is known as "the rule of three." This basically means that anything you send out magically or energetically will come back to you threefold, hence its other name, "the threefold law." This, however, is not followed in traditional witchcraft, which is less dogmatic and focuses more on folk traditions and practices. Think about the values that you wish to adhere to when practicing witchcraft, as well as the values of your home. They should reflect each other.

FOSTERING A HOUSE WITCH COMMUNITY

I'm sure at one point you've heard the word "coven" in reference to a group of witches who get together for rituals and dancing under the full moon. The basic concept is a group of witches practicing magic together. One of the joys of having a home that you feel comfortable doing magic in is opening your doors to others and do magic with them. Witchcraft is an umbrella under which many magical practices reside, and there's nothing quite like meeting other witches and learning about their magical paths and practices.

Once you've established your practice in your home, venture out and find other practitioners to learn from and make magic with. There are many online communities and groups for local witches nowadays. You can also visit your local occult, witchcraft, or metaphysical store to see if they offer meetups or classes, or take a look at their community board.

Be mindful before you throw your doors open for anyone, a little caution is wise. Get to know individuals before allowing them into your sacred space. Make sure you have a clear grasp of their intentions.

HARNESSING THE NATURAL WORLD AT HOME

While being a house witch and performing house witchery happens largely inside your home, one of the main attributes of a witch is their connection to nature. By building a relationship with nature and its spirits that we can accomplish successful spellwork. Many natural elements will strengthen the magical forces that already exist within your home. Incorporating nature into your home can be as simple as collecting a few of your favorite crystals and stones, taking care of a potted plant, or even adopting a pet.

If you have a backyard or balcony try growing herbs that are common in witchcraft, such as rosemary, mugwort, and vervain. If you don't have an outside space, or maybe you lack a green thumb, adopt a succulent to keep as a little nature spirit. Bones, taxidermy, dried foliage, and feathers also have strong ties to nature spirits and should be welcome additions to a witch's abode. You'll find as you progress in your craft and by reading this book just how vital nature will be to your practice.

The Elements

Since we've established the importance of nature in witchcraft, it stands to reason that witches work with the elements found within nature. Just because the home and hearth might be the central focus of your craft doesn't mean you should neglect the outside world entirely. On the contrary, the elements should be respected and used in your practice, regardless of which avenue of witchcraft you decide to pursue.

In the mundane world, most people are aware of four elements—earth, air, fire, and water—but witches also work with a fifth element: spirit. You can work with these elements individually or together. Some witches feel a stronger connection to one element over the others. If you love swimming, long baths, and rainy days, you may find a stronger connection to the water. On the other hand, if you love working with herbs, hiking, and animals, you may feel a closer connection to earth. Bringing the elements into your house witchery can lend additional potency to your spellwork and help you create an environment that is in harmony with the natural world.

Lunar Phases

The moon plays a significant role in rituals and spellwork. Throughout varied histories and mythologies, witches have worshipped the moon. According to *Aradia, or the Gospel of the Witches* by Charles Godfrey Leland, witches were created by Aradia, daughter of Diana the moon goddess, making witches descendants of the moon. The connection to the moon can be solidified by the fact that many of ancient civilizations' great lunar deities are also associated with witchcraft and magic, such as the Roman Diana, the Greco-Roman Hecate, and the Egyptian god Thoth.

In house witchery, the phases of the moon serve as a guide to decide which spell to cast and when, to maximize its chances of success. We will address lunar phases later in the book when we begin doing spells. If you can, download a moon phase app or buy a lunar calendar or almanac at a bookstore to use in your practice. Your local library is also a great source for material about moon phases and their role in spells and witchcraft.

The Planets and Astrological Signs

Different planets rule different aspects of magic. For example, Saturn rules witches and witchcraft, as well as the herbs associated with magic. Mercury is associated with communication, technology, and travel. Jupiter corresponds to money, wealth, and power. Astrology can be used alone or in conjunction with the lunar phases. For example, a full moon in Aquarius is prime time for love workings and spells for emotional healing. When you have a better understanding and knowledge of planets, their associations, and astrology, you can gauge the perfect time to do specific kinds of spells.

The days of the week, too, present an opportunity to time your spells just right. Each day of the week is linked to a planet, making it easier to plan out spells. For example, Sunday is *sun* day and Monday is *moon* day, so performing a spell that requires the sun's energy on a Sunday is advisable, and working a spell that requires the moon's energy on a Monday may yield the most favorable results. Remember, monitoring the planets and astrological components can enhance the potency of spells.

The Seasons

As the seasons change, so does witches' magic. Every season is linked to a different magical focus, with different celebrations and mythologies coming to the forefront. Fall and winter are linked to death and the underworld, while spring and summer are times of renewal and fertility. Think about all the changes that come with the seasons. In the colder months, the moon dominates more of the twenty-four-hour cycle, whereas during the summer months, the sun is available for more hours of the day.

Likewise, the changing seasons represent an opportunity to consider the tools and ingredients used in witchery. Using autumn as an example, some herbs that are associated with the season are rosemary, sage, and thyme. How can you incorporate those into your spellwork to honor the season and tap into its energies?

The Solar Festivals

Just as with the moon, witches have a strong connection to the sun and its powers. The sun not only casts out the shadows of darkness, but it also grants us life and nurtures our planet. The sun plays a central role in many magical practices, and many rituals and celebrations that survive today surround the sun and the need for its light. For instance, Beltane is a fire festival that is commonly held on the first of May. This is a time for bonfires to honor the sun. A similar solar festival called Dies Natalis Solis Invicti, an ancient Roman holiday, celebrated the return of the sun. It was celebrated on December 25 of each year, and many scholars speculate this was the precursor to Christmas, along with the Celtic celebration of Yule.

The Wheel of the Year

In modern paganism and Wicca, the wheel of the year helps witches synchronize their practices with seasonal changes. As a witch and practitioner of house witchery, you may want to incorporate the wheel of the year into your personal practice or at least learn about the significance of the seasons in witchcraft so that you may participate in the magical celebrations, either with a group of other witches or in the sanctuary of your own home. The wheel consists of the year's main solar events, which mark the solstices and equinoxes, and the midpoints between these days. Using the wheel of the year is a way to mark the passage of time and all that each season has traditionally represented.

Festivities on these sabbats, or festivals, tend to rely on folk traditions and vary by region but have been widely influenced by more contemporary Wiccan practices. The major sabbats are Yule (winter solstice or midwinter), Imbolc (also known as Candlemas, marking the first signs of spring), Ostara (spring equinox, marking the balance between dark and light), Beltane (or May Eve, celebrating the power of life), Litha (summer solstice), Lammas (also known as Lughnasadh, the first harvest festival of the year), Mabon (autumn equinox), and Samhain (a time for honoring the dead).

EMBRACE BEING A HOUSE WITCH

You've come so far already, but there's so much more magic and knowledge waiting for you to explore. Furthering your education in witchcraft and occult practices will only strengthen your skills as a house witch. Are you curious about a magical practice or spiritual path? If so, read up on it. Magic practices differ across cultures and regions of the world, each having its own mythology and knowledge base, offering you endless opportunities to learn and make your house witchery practice completely individualized.

The path of the witch requires dedication, not just to the practice of witchcraft, but to the spirits of nature and the household energies with which you've established a relationship. It is a path of continuously learning to honor the energies of nature, yourself, and your workings. When you claim the title of "witch," you take on the mantle of those who have not only walked this path before you, but perhaps were ostracized and even persecuted for their path. Witches have historically been the rebels and underdogs. They stand alongside the marginalized and oppressed and support those in need. This is why your home is a magical temple and sacred space. It is your fortress. Embrace your power and your house witchery.

KEY TAKEAWAYS

We've addressed a lot in this chapter. You've learned the significance of the word "home" and the importance of comfort and security in your practice, and you now know the benefits of practicing witchcraft in your home. Here are a few other things to remember from this chapter:

- Protecting your home magically also protects yourself.
- Mundane tasks like cleaning and cooking also play major roles in witchcraft and magic.
- Many everyday tools also have magical uses.
- Connecting with nature and the elements is an integral part of witchcraft.
- Use the phases of the moon to help determine the appropriate time to cast a spell.
- The seasons and witches' wheel of the year offer guidance for performing rituals and celebrating the seasons and passage of time.
- Explore social media, online groups, and local metaphysical shops to find other witches and magical practitioners.
- Invest in an almanac to keep track of lunar cycles, planetary alignments, and astrological correspondences.
- Create a deeper connection with nature and incorporate aspects of nature into your home with crystals, plants, stones, and bones.

CHAPTER 3

Preparing the Home for Magic

Now that you've learned the tenets and basics of house witchery, it's time to do some prep work before we begin performing hands-on magic. In this chapter, you will learn about the preparations and tools that are essential to witchcraft and performing house magic. We'll cover everything from what tools to add to your witch's arsenal, to creating an altar and work space, to the role that deities and spirits play in house witchery and how to build a relationship with them. Proper preparation is critical to spellwork success.

BEGIN WITH A MAGICAL FOUNDATION

Creating a sacred space is essential to performing any kind of magic. Witches should feel secure, comfortable, and safe in their environment when they are doing rituals and spells. They should feel like the space in which they perform their magic is sacred. Privacy may be a little trickier for some to achieve, but it is essential. Witchcraft is often performed in secret, which is why one of the tenets of traditional witchcraft is "to keep secret." Finding a space where you can be alone is more important than finding a space that meets your aesthetic.

Even clearing a space in a corner of your bedroom so you have enough space to lay out your tools. Additionally, allow yourself adequate time to be alone so that you can complete your magical workings.

Evaluate Your Space

If you live alone, chances are you have many spaces at your disposal to choose from, such as your bedroom, living room, kitchen, and even your backyard. If you live with others, you may want to create a space in your bedroom, and that's just fine, too. However, it's important to stop and consider what kinds of workings you'll be performing so you know how much room you'll need. That will dictate things such as how much space to clear on your floor or whether you need to move or rearrange any furniture. You want to do this before you start any workings so you don't have to interrupt your spellwork for such tasks. Remember, you want to feel comfortable and relaxed.

Clean Up and Organize

Remember when we discussed how many mundane acts also have magical correlations? This is very true when it comes to cleaning and organizing. Cleaning is a way to make your space sacred physically and ritualistically. Once you know where you'll be performing your magic, take time to clean the space, removing any papers, clothes, and other clutter that may hinder your work. If your space feels chaotic, so will your magic. Vacuum the carpet or sweep and mop the floor where you'll be standing or sitting. Make sure your surroundings look tidy so you're not distracted by messiness, and remove any other sources of distraction from your line of sight.

Cleanse and Purify

Cleansing is the spiritual act of removing negative vibrations and energies from a space, and while it's related to cleaning, it's not the same thing. Cleansing a space magically can be accomplished by various methods, the most common being via spiritual fumigation (i.e., smoke cleansing) and spiritual washes. There are many herbs and incenses that are perfect for cleansing spaces, such as frankincense, dragon's blood, rosemary, rue, and amber. These can be burned in incense form or in a dried bundle. Spiritual washes are made exclusively for cleansing spaces. They are often perfumed waters or alcohol-based liquids that are intended specifically to be sprinkled around the home or used to wash floors and windows.

Claim and Dedicate Your Sacred Space

Now that your sacred space is neat and tidy, it's time to dedicate it to the task of performing magic. This lets the house, spirits, and energies around you know your intentions for the space. Stand in the area where you'll be performing your magic or ritual. Close your eyes and take three deep breaths. Imagine a blue light surrounding yourself and the space. Whether speaking aloud or internally, say something along the lines of "I dedicate this area as my sacred space, where I will perform acts of witchcraft, magic, and sorcery. This space is shielded and protected from outside influences and is accessible only to my guides and the spirits and deities I invite within."

CARRYING OUT SMALL BUT SPIRITUAL MOMENTS

Magic is all around us, and being a witch means knowing how to tap into this magic. While we've discussed the importance of creating a sacred space for magic and ritual, not all magic has to performed in this space. Small acts of magic can be done anywhere. When you have a free moment or before doing a spell, small magical acts can help strengthen your intentions and create a powerful and spiritual moment. Following are some ways to turn otherwise mundane moments into magical ones.

- Close your eyes and take three deep breaths. This allows you to relax and clear your mind prior to doing a magical working or ritual.
- Sweep around your home, visualizing any negative or stagnant energy leaving your space.
- Sprinkle salt around your doorways and windowsills, as salt absorbs negative energy and provides protection and spiritual cleansing.
- Bathe prior to any spell or magical working. If you're taking a bath, sprinkle some Epsom salt or a few drops of essential oil into the water. For a shower, use your favorite body wash. Imagine yourself washing away any stresses or negative energies that may be clinging to you.
- Make a cup of tea. Pick out your favorite tea or choose one that might assist in whatever working you'll be performing. Make the tea and add it to your favorite mug or cup. Sweeten it to your satisfaction, stirring your spoon clockwise three times, as you imagine that you're sweetening up the day and filling the cup with love and happiness. Sip and enjoy.

THE TOOLS OF A HOUSE WITCH

Witchcraft is a hands-on practice made more effective by the right magical tools. You're probably more familiar with the tools used in witchcraft than you might think, such as the cauldron, wand, and broom. Tools are both symbolic and ritualistic. Many of the tools that witches use in spellwork are steeped in lore and mythology. For house witches, the most common and necessary tools are commonplace items. While there are many vendors, artists, and shops that carry exquisite witchcraft tools, the magic comes from you. There are many alternatives to pricey tools that won't break the bank, so put functionality above aesthetics. Following are a few of the major necessities required to start your witch's tool kit.

Shrines and Altars

Altars are primarily used for performing rituals and spells, while shrines are usually spaces dedicated to a spirit, deity, or ancestor. You can have as many altars and shrines in your home as you like, or you can have just one. You can even have portable altars and shrines. Create an altar/shrine using a small table, a bookcase, or the top of your dresser. Clear an area, drape a nice cloth over it, and use it to place candles and offerings and for any spellwork. If you are making a shrine, consider who the shrine is for. If it's for an ancestor, decorate the space with pictures and things that they enjoyed or that belonged to them. If it's for a spirit or deity, you may wish to place offerings and collect art related to them.

Cauldrons

The cauldron is a sacred vessel that represents the womb and transformation. It is associated with various goddesses around the world. Traditionally, cauldrons are made of cast iron. However, in ancient Rome, Greece, and Ireland, cauldrons made of bronze and copper were used for magic. Today, it is quite easy to find a nice cauldron to suit your witchy needs, both online and at most metaphysical shops. They come in various sizes. Be sure to find one that calls out to you and fits in your space. Make sure that it is heat safe. Avoid ceramic and glass. Your cauldron will predominantly be used to burn incense, candles, petitions, and offerings, as well as to make magical waters.

Candles and Incense

Candles are an essential part of most spells and rituals, and incense is used to cleanse sacred spaces and as an offering to spirits and deities. White and black chime candles are a good starting point, as these colors are used for protection, banishing, and wish fulfillment. As for incense, stick and cone incense are both perfect for most rituals. Frankincense is common for cleansing and for conducting spiritual work. Both candles and incense can be found online and at many metaphysical shops. Try a local botanica (Hispanic spiritual shop), or search online for an herbal apothecary for a wider variety of candles.

Crystals and Stones

Crystals are Mother Nature's batteries. They are used by witches and spiritual people alike to stay connected to nature, as well as to energize and fuel manifestations. There are a wide variety of crystals, stones, and gems, each with its own properties. Witches commonly use crystals to enhance their power, get grounded, fuel spellwork, and present as offerings to spirits and deities. Crystal shops, craft stores, and metaphysical shops all carry crystals, as do a multitude of online retailers. Choosing a crystal for a specific purpose calls for a combination of research and intuition; sometimes a crystal will call to you because it's exactly what you need.

Essential Oils

Essential oils contain the essence of specific herbs or plants. They are used to dress candles, make incense, incorporate in rituals and baths, and cast spells. Essential oils can also be mixed together to create magical blends for spellwork and magic. You can find essential oils at online retailers, most metaphysical shops, online, and even in some supermarkets, like Whole Foods. Before splurging on a multitude of different oils and fragrances, start by obtaining those that are most popular in witchcraft, such as rosemary, lavender, sandalwood, cinnamon, or rose.

If you have pets, it's important to note that many popular essential oils can be toxic when diffused into the air, so be sure to do your research. Another point worth mentioning here: Since it takes a lot of plant material to make a small amount of oil, it's always a good idea to research the company you're considering purchasing from to ensure their oils are sustainably and ethically sourced.

Kitchenware

There are a few standard items used in witchcraft that can be found in the kitchen, or at least a witch's kitchen. One of those is the mortar and pestle, a necessary tool for mixing, grinding, and smashing herbs, roots, bones, and other magical ingredients needed to make powders. Ritual bowls are used to hold offerings, water, and food for spirits and deities. A chalice is a goblet used to hold sacred beverages or water in ritual, though in a pinch, a simple wineglass will suffice.

Food and Drink

In witchcraft, food and drink are often part of spells and rituals, as well as aftercare practices. Food and drink are usually saved for offerings to deities, household spirits, and ancestors but can also be used for rituals related to holidays. In most covens, witches feast after rituals to ground and replenish their energy. This is a good practice for solitary practitioners, because spellwork can use a lot of energy, leaving you drained. Wine, cider, and juice can be used as offerings to spirits and deities. Foods such as bread, cheese, berries, honey, and chocolate make good offerings, too.

Herbs

Herbs are as integral to witchcraft as gas is to cars. Herbs contain energy that fuels spells. They are the magical conduit to mother earth. Herbs are used in charm bags, spiritual baths, magical powders, and more. Many herbs that are common in cooking are also essential to witchcraft, such as rosemary, thyme, cinnamon, pepper, oregano, and basil. You can find many herbs at your local grocery store and more obscure herbs, such as mugwort, can be sourced from metaphysical stores, online witchcraft shops, and herbal supply stores.

Plants

While an herb is any plant that has nutritional or medicinal purposes, the word "plant" refers more generally to any member of the plant kingdom. Like herbs, plants are some of witches' greatest allies, with power to heal us both spiritually and physically. Plants support us in life-critical ways, such as by creating oxygen. Without the plant world, we would not be here. Besides that, plants offer us energy, wisdom, and cheer. For house witchery, it would be wise to have a few potted plants that thrive indoors. Choose a hardy plant that does well in shade, or multitask with a plant like rosemary, which is also an herb that is useful in a variety of spells and rituals. Go to your local garden store and see what magical plant catches your eye, then name it and care for it. Now you have your own plant familiar.

Grimoire

The grimoire is a witch's personal book of magical workings. It is useful for writing down spells you've learned or developed on your own. It's a lot like a cookbook, filled with your personal knowledge about magic, spells, magical correspondences, and rituals. You can buy a journal, use a folder or binder, or create your own bound book. The point is that this is a highly individualized record of your journey as a witch. There are many wonderful blank grimoires available on Etsy and elsewhere online. Find one that speaks to you.

Deities to Aid in Home Witchcraft

Now that we've explored some of the tools used in the craft, let us explore the deities tied to household magic and witchcraft. There are a number of deities from different civilizations that are associated with the home and hearth. Many of them come from ancient Greece, Rome, and Egypt. Norse and Celtic religions that are no longer practiced today also believed in some ancient deities that have been revived by some pagan sects.

Before you begin your work with deities, make sure to do your research. Learn about their history, background, and preferred ways of paying homage to them. Do your due diligence before working with any deities that aren't from your own culture so that you can be sure you aren't appropriating anything that is considered sacred.

While deities have been known to offer protection and assistance, they are not there to serve you, nor are they *required* to assist in your spells or magical workings. It's very important to be in a deity's good graces, so making respectful offerings and taking time to learn about them are essential. Find out what you can about the folklore and mythologies surrounding the deities you want to invite into your space. The deities that follow are a few of the most helpful ones with whom I personally recommend getting acquainted.

Bes

Hailing from Nubia, a region of Egypt, Bes is usually depicted as a dwarf and is the protector of households. He is also known to look after children and mothers and to drive off evil spirits. Invoke Bes when you need protection, wish to purge your house of negative energy, or want to ward off spirits, negative vibes, and toxic people. Keep an image of Bes by your bed or entrance to your home to keep troublesome spirits away. Honor Bes by offering a small knife or instrument, such as a tambourine, as a gift.

Brigid/Brigitte

The Celtic goddess of hearth and home, Brigid is also the goddess of healing, poetry, art, prophecy, and livestock. She is the matron goddess of artists and philosophers. Invoke Brigid for spells and rituals concerning healing, wisdom, career success, and love. Her sacred number is nine, and a white candle burned in her name represents the eternal flame that was kept in her temple at Kildare. She is associated with the cauldron, snakes, and white cows. Offer her blackberries, milk, ale, eggs, white candles, and coins. The first of February, also known as Imbolc, is her sacred day.

Hecate/Hekate

While commonly known today as the goddess of witchcraft and the moon, Hecate's Greco-Roman origins are actually those of a household goddess. In ancient Greece, it was common to have a small statue or plaque of Hecate by the hearth to protect the home from evil spirits. Invoke Hecate for justice, especially having to do with physical crimes or abuse.

Hecate may also be invoked for the protection of dogs and for communicating with spirits. Keys, cauldrons, and brooms are all sacred tools of Hecate. Her traditional offerings and sacred plants are garlic, pomegranate, mandrake, yew, and dates. The last Friday of every month was traditionally dedicated to her.

Hestia/Vesta

The Greek Hestia, who was called Vesta in Rome, is a goddess of the hearth and home. She represents fire, especially that which is used in the hearth or during ritual. She protects all those who dwell within the home and can be invoked for safety, peace, and respect. Lit candles are wonderful offerings to Hestia/Vesta. Simply light them and say her name to burn them in her honor. While the two goddesses are often thought of as one and the same, the Roman Vesta is much older and was venerated in Italy long before Hestia made an appearance in Greece. In ancient Rome, virtually every sacrifice, ritual, and offering was dedicated to her before any other deity.

Juno

Juno is the Roman goddess of marriage, fertility, motherhood, households, and domestic living. She is one of the oldest Roman deities, and in some myths, she is the spirit of time, controlling the calendar and women's menstrual cycles. While she is a household goddess and can be invoked by anyone, she has a stronger connection to women and children. Invoke her for spells related to fertility, healing, marriage, and mending heartbreak. When invoking Juno, use peacock feathers or imagery of such feathers in your spellwork. The first day of every month is dedicated to Juno, and her sacred months are June and February.

Lares

Revered in every household in the Roman Republic during its reign, lares are household guardians who protect the family, their land, and their property. Lares are benevolent spirits that reside within every dwelling, living alongside us in harmony. Ancient Romans kept altars dedicated to the lares in their homes, usually featuring statues or images of the lares or of two snakes, their sacred animal. Honor the lares when you cleanse or bless the home before guests and family come to visit and when you need protection. Keep an image of them or snakes to represent them in your household altar.

HONORING HOUSEHOLD SPIRITS AND GUARDIANS

Household spirits like the lares are found in countless civilizations and cultures. Throughout history, we have shared our homes with spirits, both primordial and ancestral. These spirits of the home aren't like formal deities in the sense that they aren't worshipped and part of a specific pantheon, but they are prominent in folklore, legends, and myths, and therefore they should be acknowledged and respected just the same. You may already be familiar with some of these spirits, such as goblins, elves, and brownies. However, these are only a few of the many such spirits known to dwell invisibly alongside us. Building a relationship with household spirits is essential to your house witchery, as we need spirit allies to produce successful magic. Many of these household spirits are linked to specific cultures and regions. I suggest familiarizing yourself with the origins of specific household spirits and their native cultures. A wonderful resource for spirits and deities is the *Encyclopedia of Spirits* by Judika Illes.

TRANSFORMING YOUR HOME WITH WITCHCRAFT

You have now gained the knowledge and information about the tools you need and are ready to begin performing spellwork, rituals, and house witchery. Doing spellwork is no easy task, but the feeling of casting a spell is truly something that is hard to explain, especially when you get confirmation of the spell's success.

Performing spellwork and rituals allows you to take full control of a situation and your household. You become your own master and control your own fate. The house becomes your temple. Now that you are ready to perform witchcraft in your home, here's what you have to look forward to:

- Create magical blends to transform mundane cleaning into magical cleaning.
- Learn how to make magical oils, salves, powders, and teas.
- Attract household spirits.
- Banish unwanted spirits.
- Make magical talismans and charms.
- Stop gossip during a dinner party.
- Mend broken friendships.
- Create protection charms and cast spells.

KEY TAKEAWAYS

It's time to cast some spells! Before we grab our broomsticks, let's revisit what we learned in this chapter, as it is essential to your spellcraft.

- Prepare your house and environment so that it is ready for spells and rituals.
- Cleanse your space prior to performing magic via spiritual fumigation.
- Clean and organize your space. Remember, cluttered space leads to cluttered magic.
- Take time daily for little personal rituals prior to performing magic, such as bathing, breathing deeply, and making and enjoying a cup of tea.
- Start gathering tools and materials for your witch's arsenal. Get yourself a nice broom, cauldron, and chalice to use during spells and rituals.
- Familiarize yourself with different crystals, gems, and stones and their properties.
- Raid your kitchen cupboard and see what herbs and spices you have that could be useful in witchery.
- Go to your local grocery store or farmers' market and invest in some herbs.
- Get yourself a plant familiar for your home.
- Acknowledge and honor the spirits of the home.
- Read up on various household deities and see which ones call to you.
- Leave an offering or set up an altar/shrine to a deity or spirit that appeals to you.
- Research household spirits and learn about their cultural backgrounds.

PART II

Spells, Rituals, and Remedies for a Magical Home

This section of the book is a grimoire, a magical tome filled with spells, remedies, and rituals to assist in your house witchery. Within these pages, you will find spells to drive away negative spirits, attract abundance, stop gossip, purify sacred space, and bring in luck and happiness. Many have been passed down through history and survived through folklore and secondhand accounts. Some come straight from my personal grimoire, while others were shared with me by mentors. These spells are meant to be performed within the home to help you create a magical household and a magical way of life.

CHAPTER 4

Cleansing the Home

Spiritual cleansing should be done before any magical act as a way of purging negative or unwanted energies that can be parasitic in nature. This chapter includes rituals and spells intended to help cleanse your home of negative energies, as well as remedies to clean up physical dirt and grime. A witch's home doesn't have to be spotless or free of dirt and debris. However, it should be clear of stagnant energy and spiritual gunk. Many spells and remedies for cleansing share similar herbs and ingredients, such as citrus and vinegar, as these are used in both the magical and mundane worlds. Cleansing the household allows room for more benevolent energies and helpful spirits.

ANCIENT ASPERGING CLEANSING

Asperging is the sprinkling of liquid to spiritually cleanse and purify. This ancient rite has been performed for centuries by many different civilizations, including ancient Egyptians, Greeks, Romans, and Celts. The act of sprinkling can be done by using your fingers to sprinkle the liquid or by using an herb branch. This liquid-based cleansing is also a preferred method for those who don't wish to burn herbs or are sensitive to smoke and strong aromas.

MATERIALS

Small bowl
Water
Pinch salt
3 pinches rosemary (dried or fresh)

INSTRUCTIONS

1. Fill a small bowl with water.
2. Add the salt.
3. Add the rosemary.
4. Close your eyes, take a deep breath, and gently blow into the bowl, imagining it filling with bright light as you do so.
5. Place both your hands over the bowl of water and say aloud or internally: *"I purify this sacred water. May it cleanse my home and sacred space."*
6. Walk around your home holding the bowl in your hands, and with your left hand, sprinkle the water on your living space's corners, windowsills, and doorways.
7. Pour the remainder of the water over your hands in the sink when you have finished sprinkling the sacred water around your space.

WITCH'S BROOM CLEANSING SPELL

It's time to use the broom for magic! This cleansing spell is quite old and simple, yet it gets the job done. Brooms have a long history with spiritual cleansing and magic. Here, we use the broom for both its household and magical functions.

MATERIALS

Broom
Dustpan
Pinch salt

INSTRUCTIONS

1. Sweep the floor of your space with the broom, starting at the back of your home, away from the entrance and moving toward the front.
2. Say aloud or internally as you sweep: *"Sacred broom, sweep the bad away and protect this home another day."*
3. Sweep dust and debris into the dustpan.
4. Toss the dust outside your front door. If you cannot do this, wash it down the sink or toilet. (Do not toss debris/dust in the house trash can or bin, as you do not want that energy remaining in the home.)
5. Take your broom and place it by the entrance of your home, bristles facing up.
6. Sprinkle the salt over the bristles and say: *"Salt of the earth, enchant my broom. Cleanse it from the energies it swept up in this room."*

ARCHANGEL SPACE CLEANSING RITUAL

Archangels in witchcraft? Yes, you read that right. Archangels are strong spiritual agents that are often used in ceremonial magic to clear spaces and are invoked in many rituals for protection during spellwork. This basic concept of ritual is actually one I was first introduced to by my grandmother when I was a child, but it can be found in spiritual practices such as Santeria, hoodoo, Southern conjure, ceremonial magic, and traditional witchcraft. This ritual requires no tools; however, you may wish to burn some incense, such as frankincense, as an offering to these otherworldly spirits.

INSTRUCTIONS

1. Stand in the center of the home, room, or space you wish to cleanse. Each archangel will be summoned to watch over a certain point of your household.
2. Take three deep breaths, close your eyes, and envision a bright blue light encircling your sacred space.
3. Open your eyes, turn to the east, and say: *"Raphael to the east, cleanse and purify."*
4. Turn to the south and say: *"Michael to the south, cleanse and purify."*
5. Turn to the west and say: *"Gabriel to the west, cleanse and purify."*
6. Turn to the north and say: *"Uriel to the north, cleanse and purify."*
7. Take a deep breath, close your eyes, and say: *"Archangels cleanse my space, and let my home be a purified place."*
8. Thank and acknowledge the angels for their assistance.

DRAGON'S BLOOD CLEANSING

Dragon's blood is used to neutralize and exorcise negative energies and spirits. It was used to cleanse space in ancient Roman rituals and in medieval European ceremonial magic. Dragon's blood is a resin that can be found in many metaphysical shops, as well as online. It can be purchased in many different forms, such as stick incense, but for this remedy, we will be using resin chunks.

MATERIALS

Dragon's blood resin chunks
Mortar and pestle
Self-lighting charcoal disk
Heat-safe bowl or dish (metal or ceramic)
Lighter or matches

INSTRUCTIONS

1. Place a few chunks of the dragon's blood in the mortar. Use the pestle to mash and grind it down as best you can until it's fully powdered.
2. Place the charcoal disk in the bowl and light the disk; wait for it to spark a bit.
3. Put the dish in the center of the space you wish to cleanse.
4. Take a pinch of the powdered dragon's blood and sprinkle it on top of the burning charcoal disk.
5. Waft the smoke to different areas of the space with your left hand, envisioning the area being cleared of stagnant and unwanted energies. Add more powder as necessary.

GARLIC CLEANSING REMEDY

The enemy of the vampire and a very potent cleanser, garlic is used in many folk magic spells to cleanse, banish, and protect. It's used from the Carpathian Mountains of Romania to the swampland of South Florida, where I grew up and where many Cubans practice Santeria. This folk remedy derives from a Cuban formula I learned, but similar variations of the same remedy are found in many different cultures and spiritual practices. Use this remedy when you wish to rid your space of psychic vampires or you want to purge your space of residual energy from others that might be hanging about.

MATERIALS

3 garlic cloves, peeled
Mortar and pestle
Pinch brown sugar
Self-lighting charcoal disk
Heat-safe bowl or dish
Lighter or matches

INSTRUCTIONS

1. Place the garlic in the mortar, and add the brown sugar.
2. Use the pestle to grind and pound the brown sugar and garlic together, mixing thoroughly.
3. Place the charcoal disk in the dish, and light the disk.
4. Sprinkle the garlic and sugar mixture onto the charcoal disk.
5. Using your left hand, waft the smoke over the areas you wish to cleanse.

CONJURE CLEANSING FLOOR WASH

Floor washes are a prime example of physical house cleaning combined with magic. Floor washes are popular in spiritual practices such as Southern conjure (a mixture of magical traditions from Africa, Native American tribes, and different parts of Europe), hoodoo, and North American folk magic. This recipe comes from a dear friend who lives in New Orleans. This multitasking household magic is not only extremely potent, but also subtle and discreet—the perfect way to cleanse your space, especially if you're living with others in the household.

MATERIALS

- Large mopping bucket
- Warm water
- 1 tablespoon salt
- 1 teaspoon rosemary
- 1 teaspoon agrimony
- 1 cup white vinegar
- 6 drops peppermint essential oil
- Mop and rag

INSTRUCTIONS

1. Fill the bucket with warm water.
2. Add the salt, rosemary, and agrimony.
3. Pour in the vinegar and peppermint oil.
4. Mix the ingredients together until they are well blended.
5. Use the mop and rag to wash the floor, as well as countertops, chairs, windowsills, or other surfaces you wish to clean.
6. Allow the washed surfaces to air-dry so that the power of the magical botanicals and ingredients permeates into the area that needs to be cleansed.
7. Pour the remaining mixture out your back door or in your backyard, or flush it down the toilet.

JASMINE AND PEPPERMINT BOTANICAL CLEANSING SPRAY

You will love the aroma of these combined botanicals. Between the protective properties of peppermint and the cleansing powers of jasmine, this spray is sure to eradicate any stagnant or malevolent energies that may be lingering in your home. It will also create a soothing atmosphere. Use this spray whenever you wish to change up the energies in the home.

MATERIALS

Empty spray bottle
Water
Pinch salt
3 drops peppermint oil
4 drops jasmine oil

INSTRUCTIONS

1. Fill the spray bottle with water.
2. Add the salt, peppermint oil, and jasmine oil.
3. Screw the cap onto the bottle and shake the bottle vigorously.
4. Mist the corners and perimeter of the space you wish to cleanse.
5. Store the remaining mixture in a cool, dark place when not in use.

CRYSTAL VACUUM CLEANERS

This simple ritual can be done as often as you find necessary. Crystals such as amethyst and other quartz varieties are known to absorb stagnant or malevolent energies. The clear quartz will purify the energies of those who enter your household. Selenite is known to absorb unhelpful energies and amplify the positive properties of other crystals, as well as to cleanse and recharge other crystals.

MATERIALS

1 piece amethyst
1 piece clear quartz
2 pieces selenite

INSTRUCTIONS

1. Place the amethyst in the bedroom where you sleep, either under your bed or by your nightstand.
2. Place the quartz by the entrance of your home.
3. Place the two pieces of selenite in different corners of your home. Keep the crystals there as long as you like, but recharge them with salt water every few months.

SACRED SALT SPELL

Salt is a key ingredient in witchcraft and magic. It absorbs negative energy, drives away malefic spirits, and purifies and protects sacred spaces. This simple spell is perfect for quick and discreet energy cleansing and can also be done prior to any ritual or spellwork.

MATERIALS

Small glass jar

Salt (enough to fill jar)

INSTRUCTIONS

1. Fill the glass jar with salt. This will be your personal reserve for cleansing, protection, and spellwork.
2. Place your hands over the jar, close your eyes, and say aloud or internally: *"Salt of the earth, protect and cleanse for me, as I will so mote it be."*
3. Sprinkle around and throughout your home to absorb negativity and clear bad energies.
4. Repeat the spell once a week, monthly, or during every full moon.

BLUE CHIME CANDLE CLEANSING

This candle spell may be tiny, but it's potent. Chime candles are made specifically for magic and rituals, and they burn for between one and two hours. The color blue is often associated with healing, cleansing, and purification in witchcraft and folk magic. Olive oil is also used in magic to bless and cleanse sacred objects and spaces and serves as an offering to deities and spirits. Use this spell when you wish to fumigate stagnant energies or during the beginning of each month for a fresh new start.

MATERIALS

1 drop virgin olive oil
1 blue chime candle
Chime candleholder (optional)
Lighter or matches

INSTRUCTIONS

1. Place the olive oil in your palm and **anoint** the candle, rubbing the oil all over the candle to cover it thoroughly.
2. Place the candle in the candleholder (if using) and put the candle in the space you wish to cleanse. If you don't have a chime candleholder, get creative. For instance, a wineglass may do the trick.
3. Light the candle and say aloud or internally: *"Sacred flame burning bright, cleanse this space with your light."*
4. Allow the candle to burn down completely, making sure that you keep an eye on it.

EGG SPACE CLEANSING

Eggs are quite prominent in witchcraft and folk magic. They are known to be highly absorbent and are often used in cleansing to vacuum up negative debris and psychic energy, as well as to break **hexes** and curses. Implement this egg cleansing when you feel negative energy lingering in your home, whether after a fight, when you feel anxious, or if you feel someone is sending bad vibes your way. This cleansing is twofold in that it will cleanse both you and your space.

MATERIALS

1 egg

Brown paper bag

INSTRUCTIONS

1. Hold the egg in both hands, close your eyes, and envision the egg beaming with white light.
2. Gently rub the egg all over your body, being careful not to crack it.
3. Hide the egg inside your home in a spot where it will not be disturbed, roll away, or break.
4. Retrieve the egg from its hiding spot after twenty-four hours have passed, and place it in the brown paper bag.
5. Discard the bag away from your home so that the absorbed energy does not linger in your sacred space.

CHARMED CLEANSING OIL

Rosemary was regarded as a sacred herb by the ancient Romans, offering protection from malefic energies, as well as in war and combat. Rosemary was also used to cleanse sacred space, along with other magical botanicals, such as thyme and sandalwood. Use this oil blend to cleanse your magical tools, candles, and sacred space. Storing it in an amber glass bottle keeps the oil blend protected from ultraviolet rays that can degrade the mixture. Pour a few drops in your bath or rub it on your body when you wish to cleanse yourself.

MATERIALS

- 1½ ounces olive oil
- 1 small (2-ounce) amber glass bottle
- 6 drops rosemary essential oil
- 4 drops sandalwood essential oil
- 2 drops thyme essential oil

INSTRUCTIONS

1. Pour the olive oil into the bottle.
2. Add the rosemary, sandalwood, and thyme essential oils to the bottle.
3. Screw on the cap and shake the mixture vigorously.
4. Keep the bottle in a cool, dark place when not in use.

Salt

CHAPTER 5

Purifying the Home

Purification is the ceremonial act of making something clean or renewed. This is probably one of the oldest forms of magic and ritual. Purifying space prior to performing any sort of religious act dates back to ancient Egypt, when priests would spiritually fumigate temples and bathe before daily prayers and sacred rites. Most, if not all, schools of magic believe in the act of purification prior to performing spellwork. These beliefs were followed heavily in ancient Greek, Roman, and Egyptian practices and continue to be carried out by those who follow neopagan religions such as Wicca. The spells and rituals in this chapter are intended to be performed before any form of house witchery or whenever you feel you a need to spiritually boost your space and make it feel more sacred.

KHERNIPS: LUSTRAL WATER

There are certain things we do in daily life that create a sort of spiritual debris. This is similar to dirt we collect by simply being out in the world. The ancient Greeks called this "miasma," a sort of shell or armor that makes it harder to connect with our magic as well as commune with deities and spirits. This is why we cleanse ourselves before going into temples and sacred sites: to purify ourselves and get ready to connect with the divine, free from psychic muck and debris. Khernips is an ancient purifying agent meant to be used prior to ritual and magic.

MATERIALS

Spring water
Medium bowl
Pinch sea salt
3 bay leaves
Lighter or matches
1 cloth
Bottle, jar, or bowl with lid

INSTRUCTIONS

1. Pour enough spring water into the bowl to mix without spilling.
2. Sprinkle in the sea salt.
3. Hold the bay leaves together in your hand and use the lighter to set them on fire.
4. Allow the leaves to burn for several seconds, and then dunk them into the water, quenching the flames.
5. Say aloud: *"Xerniptosai"* (pronounced, "zer-nip-tos-aye-ee," meaning "be purified").

6. Leaving the bay leaves floating in the water, wash your hands and face with the newly made lustral water and say: *"I purify myself with lustral water."*
7. Sprinkle the lustral water around the areas in your space that you wish to purify and say: *"Begone, begone ye profane!"*
8. Dry your hands and face with the cloth. You may now perform your desired spell or ritual.
9. Store the remaining khernips in the lidded container and use it prior to every ritual and formal prayer. You can also sprinkle the khernips over any item that you wish to purify.

HESTIA'S HOME PURIFICATION RITUAL

Purify your home just like the ancient Greeks did with this two-thousand-year-old ritual. This ritual calls on Hestia, the goddess of hearth and home, and purifies the space around you, making it sacred and ready for further types of magic and spellwork.

MATERIALS

Bowl
Khernips (see pages 70–71)
Cloth or towel
1 self-lighting charcoal disk
Heat-safe bowl or dish
Lighter or matches
Frankincense resin incense
Myrrh resin incense

INSTRUCTIONS

1. Fill a bowl with the khernips. Use the khernips to wash your hands and face, then dry yourself off with the cloth.
2. Place the charcoal disk into the heat-safe dish. Light the disk, allowing it to burn for a few seconds, and then sprinkle the frankincense and myrrh resin incense onto the disk.
3. Invoke Hestia as the incense begins to smoke, asking for her blessing by saying aloud or internally: *"Hestia, great goddess of hearth and home, draw near, and bestow grace upon my dwelling."*
4. Grab the dish and use your free hand to waft the incense smoke in different directions of your home to fumigate your space.

5. As you do this, say: *"Goddess Hestia, venerable guardian of the unwavering flame, bless my home. Blessed Hestia, first and last, strong, stable basis of the mortal race, banish negative energies and entities from this dwelling. May love and peace reside here always!"*
6. Let the incense burn out completely.
7. Flush any remaining incense and charcoal debris down the toilet.
8. Thank Hestia for purifying your sacred space.

RING THAT BELL PURIFICATION SPELL

As simple as it may sound, bells are quite effective at clearing and purifying space. As a matter of fact, that is one of their key roles in churches. The ringing of a metal bell is disturbing to malefic spirits and entities while also attracting benevolent spirits and calling on your guides.

MATERIALS

Metal bell

INSTRUCTIONS

1. Starting at the entrance of your home, walk through your entire home ringing the bell.
2. Go through every part of the space, making sure you ring the bell in every room.
3. In between ringing the bell, say aloud or internally: *"When you hear the knell of this sacred bell, I clear the way so malevolent spirits can no longer dwell."*
4. Imagine your space being purified and cleansed by a bright blue light as you continue ringing the bell throughout each room.

BYE-BYE BANISHING POWDER

To purify a space, we must rid the area of unwanted spirits and lingering energies from toxic or negative people. This potent banishing powder is popular in American folk magic, where it is often called "Hot Foot Powder." It uses strong banishing botanicals such as cayenne pepper and black pepper to send those unwanted energies flying along.

MATERIALS

1 tablespoon black pepper
1 tablespoon cayenne pepper
1 tablespoon salt
1 tablespoon sulfur
Mortar and pestle
Glass bottle or jar

INSTRUCTIONS

1. Grind the black pepper, cayenne pepper, salt, and sulfur together to form a powder using the mortar and pestle.
2. Sprinkle a little bit of the powder along windowsills, doorways, walls, and the entrance and exit of your home.
3. Store any leftover powder in the bottle or jar for future use.

SALT AND SPELT PURIFICATION

The ancient Romans were committed to spiritual purification. Many of the purification rituals we use today have Roman origins. Spelt is a type of grain similar to rye and barley that was used in offerings and purification rituals. Today, you can find it in some artisan breads. This purification rite is useful whenever you need to rid your home or space of strong negative vibrations. Sprinkle this magical combo after a heated argument, breakup, emotional upheaval, or death. You may prepare this mixture ahead of time and store it in a jar for when you need it.

MATERIALS

2 cups salt
1 cup spelt flour or grain
Bowl
Jar

INSTRUCTIONS

1. Pour the salt into the bowl, then add the spelt.
2. Mix the contents together with your fingers and say aloud or internally: *"Salt and spelt combine into one. As I wish it, let it be done."*
3. Walk through your space, sprinkling the mixture along windowsills, doorways, corners of rooms, and entryways.
4. Say aloud or internally as you sprinkle your mixture: *"Salt and spelt purify my space. Banish all negativity from my sacred space."*
5. Pour the remainder of the mixture into the jar and save it for when you need it again.

FLORIDA WATER PERFUME PURIFICATION

Despite its name, Florida water is not actually from Florida. It's a cologne that was created in New York City in the early 1800s. Today it's made in Hong Kong. The name is derived from the mythical fountain of youth that folklore claims is somewhere in Florida. The name also comes from the Spanish word *florido,* which means "full of flowers" or "flowery." You can find Florida water online, in Hispanic markets, or at some drug stores, as well as in most metaphysical shops. While there are many methods of using Florida water for purification, here's one that I personally like.

MATERIALS

1 bottle Florida water

Bowl

Cloth

INSTRUCTIONS

1. Pour the Florida water into the bowl.
2. Dip the cloth into the bowl and use the cloth to wipe down the doors, windows, and any other surfaces you wish to purify.
3. Once you've finished wiping down the targeted surfaces, sprinkle the remaining Florida water from the bowl into the corners of your home.
4. Take a hot shower, imagining yourself being purified as you do.
5. Sprinkle some Florida water from the bottle onto your body once you've finished showering and drying off.

KITCHEN WITCHIN' PURIFICATION POTION

Many powerful plants in magic and witchcraft masquerade in the day-to-day world as common produce. Interestingly enough, some of the most popular culinary herbs are actually prized ingredients in the witch's arsenal. This purification technique combines both the magic of the home and the kitchen.

MATERIALS

Bowl
Water
3 sprigs fresh rosemary
3 sprigs fresh dill or parsley
3 sprigs fresh thyme
Cutting board or paper towel
Scissors
String, yarn, or cord

INSTRUCTIONS

1. Fill the bowl with water.
2. Lay the herbs on a dry, clean surface, such as a cutting board or paper towel.
3. Use the scissors to cut a length of string about twelve inches long.
4. Bundle all the herbs together.
5. Wrap the string around the base of the herbs six times and knot it together.
6. Use the scissors to cut the excess string.
7. Dip the herb bundle in the bowl of water. Use the herbs to sprinkle the water around the areas you wish to purify.

8. Say aloud or internally as you purify your space: *"Herbs of the witch, purify this space, and banish negativity from this sacred place."*
9. Continue sprinkling the water throughout the house in this manner until you've used all the water in the bowl.
10. Hang the bundle of herbs upside down in your kitchen and allow it to dry to ward off malefic energies and protect the home.
11. Use pieces of the herb bundle for protection, cleansing, and purification spells.

VINEGAR PURIFICATION BOWL

Not only does vinegar have its uses in physical cleaning, but this natural purifier has also long been associated with magic and witchcraft. Want to purge your space of psychic debris and have your home feeling new? Use this magical remedy, and within twenty-four hours, your home will be vibin' with positivity and a renewed freshness.

MATERIALS

1 cup white vinegar
½ cup Florida water
Bowl

INSTRUCTIONS

1. Pour the vinegar into the bowl.
2. Add the Florida water and mix gently.
3. Place the bowl in the corner of the house or space you wish to purify and say: *"Absorb the bad and purify this space. Let all bad energies leave this place."*
4. Let the bowl sit for twenty-four hours.
5. Pour the contents of the bowl into your toilet.
6. Repeat this process as needed.

CIRCE'S PURIFICATION RITUAL BATH

Circe is an ancient Greek demigoddess and sorceress best known for her appearance in Homer's *Odyssey*. She is known as the first witch in antiquity. When Jason and Medea fled Colchis, it was Circe who purified them and absolved them spiritually of their past transgressions. You learned before about miasma and being spiritually blocked by energetic debris (see page 70). This ritual bath is perfect for days when you feel spiritually blocked, angry, or sad or when everything seems to be amiss. Perform this ritual to regain your power and renew your inner witch.

MATERIALS

3 drops lavender essential oil
3 drops frankincense essential oil
3 drops rosemary essential oil
1 teaspoon olive oil

INSTRUCTIONS

1. Draw yourself a warm bath, making sure the temperature is to your liking yet cool enough that you can submerge yourself.
2. Add each of the essential oils and say aloud or internally: *"Great witch Circe of antiquity, in this bath, please purify me."*
3. Use your hand to mix the essential oils into the water.
4. Add the olive oil to the bath and say aloud or internally: *"Sacred oils bewitched by me, purify me in the name of Circe."*
5. Get into the tub, allowing yourself to get comfortable and relax.
6. Stay in the tub for at least fifteen minutes, inhaling the smell of the essential oils as you imagine the vapors surrounding you in white light and purifying you.
7. Rinse yourself off in the shower, feeling energized and renewed, both magically and physically.

DRAGON'S BLOOD PURIFICATION CHARM

Charm bags are not only an old form of magic but also a staple in witchcraft. They are easy to create, and they are a discreet way of displaying your craft. This specific charm bag works almost like an air filter, absorbing psychic debris and purifying the air. Plus, it also repels unwanted spirits.

MATERIALS

1 tablespoon dragon's blood resin
1 tablespoon salt
3 bay leaves
1 red felt or cotton pouch

INSTRUCTIONS

1. Place the dragon's blood, salt, and bay leaves into the pouch.
2. Hold the bag in both your hands and say aloud or internally: *"Sacred bag, purify my space. Let the power of the dragon protect my space."*
3. Hang the bag by the entryway of the home or dedicated space you wish to cleanse.
4. Change or discard your charm bag after three months.

MAGIC MIRROR ON THE WALL

We witches love our mirrors. Look at the Evil Queen in *Snow White*: That mirror was her bestie. Mirrors are known to trap unwanted spirits, as well as break curses and send back hexes. Why not transform your simple mirror into a purification portal? This simple remedy allows you to turn any mirror in your home into a constant purification machine.

MATERIALS

Bowl
Water
Pinch dried mugwort
Pinch dried rosemary
Pinch salt
Cloth or towel

INSTRUCTIONS

1. Fill the bowl with water.
2. Add the mugwort, rosemary, and salt to the water.
3. Mix the ingredients in the water, stirring with your index finger as you say: *"Sacred herbs of sorcery, perform my will, so mote it be."*
4. Dip the cloth into the herbal mixture and wash and wipe down all the mirrors in your home, or focus on whichever one you like the best.
5. Stare at your reflection and say: *"Mirror, mirror in this place, purify my home and space."*
6. Pour the remaining water in the sink or toilet.

BRIGID'S SACRED HEARTH CANDLE

Brigid is the Celtic goddess of the hearth and home. She was venerated by the Catholics and became St. Brigid. Upon finding her way to the Caribbean in the late eighteenth century, she transformed into Maman Brigitte, the Vodou spirit of death and protection. This candle combines all three of her sacred forms and is burned to purge your home of any and all negative energies, purifying your space with Brigid's enchanting flame. This **novena** candle becomes a symbolic representation of the hearth. Burn it in the living area to invite benevolent spirits and house guardians.

MATERIALS

- 1 gold permanent marker or paint pen
- 1 black or white glass pillar/novena candle
- Pinch cayenne pepper
- Pinch rosemary
- 3 whole cloves
- 3 drops frankincense oil
- Scissors
- Lighter or matches

INSTRUCTIONS

1. Use the marker or paint pen to draw an equal-armed cross on the glass of the candle.
2. Write the name "Brigid" three times, line by line, beneath the cross.
3. Sprinkle the cayenne pepper on top of the candle and say: *"Brigid with your sacred fire, to purify this space is my desire."*
4. Sprinkle the rosemary on the candle and say: *"This home is my temple and my sacred space."*

5. Add the cloves and say: *"With my magic and sorcery I protect this place."*
6. Add the frankincense to the candle and say: *"This candle is made in Brigid's name."*
7. Use the scissors to trim the wick, making sure not to cut it too short.
8. Light the candle and say: *"Dear Brigid, purify this space with your sacred flame."*
9. Allow the candle to burn down completely. If you cannot stay with the candle until it burns out, snuff the flame out and relight it when you return.

CHAPTER 6

Protecting the Home

This chapter will cover one of the most popular aspects of house witchery: protection. This form of magic is used to safeguard the witch and home from outside spiritual attacks, bad luck, spiritual danger, and malevolent spirits. You will also find spells and charms to repel malefic forces and deter those who wish to rob or infiltrate your home. Using witchcraft for protection will create an aura around you and your home that will enhance your safety, though it cannot defy the physical laws of nature or another person's will. So, while you can and should use magic for protection, you should also take additional steps to protect your home, such as locking your doors and windows and using an alarm.

RUE THE DAY SPELL PROTECTION

Rue is a powerful protection botanical used in witchcraft and folk magic. In Stregheria, Italian witchcraft, rue is one of the prime herbs used. It is also sacred to the ancient Roman goddess Diana and her daughter Aradia, known as the queen of the witches. Rue was such an important herb for protection that Italians made it into a protection amulet called the cimaruta, a silver image of rue. The term "rue the day" is said to come from the practice of throwing rue at enemies and those you wish to banish. While simple, this spell also offers maximum spiritual protection against trespassers and those with ill intent. You can find fresh rue at most Hispanic and Asian markets, or you can get a plant from your local garden store, nursery, or any online apothecary.

MATERIALS

1 cup water
Medium bowl
1 bundle fresh rue
Scissors
Twine or string

INSTRUCTIONS

1. Pour the water into the bowl.
2. Take the bundle of rue in your hand and dunk one end into the water.
3. Shake and fling the water around your home, sprinkling the water on walls, corners, windows, and doorways.
4. As you do this, say aloud or internally *"Goddess Diana, protect this place. With this rue, I secure my space."*

5. Use the scissors to cut a twelve-inch piece of twine. Tie this to the end of the rue once you have finished sprinkling the rue throughout your home.
6. Hang the rue upside down by the entrance or exit to your home or by a window.
7. Say aloud or internally: *"Sacred herb, hear what I say. Let those who trespass rue the day."*
8. Redo this spell as often as you like, waiting at least one month or so for the rue to dry completely.

FIVE-FINGER GRASS PROTECTION CHARM

Five-finger grass is also known as cinquefoil. The great fifteenth-century occultist Heinrich Cornelius Agrippa said it could "drive away devils." Not only is five-finger grass a powerful banishing agent, but it is also used in spells for prophecy and astral travel, making this herb a prized possession among witches. Make this charm on a Wednesday during the hours of 5 p.m., 7 p.m., or 9 p.m. to attract the spirit of Mercury and maximize the protective energies of the charm. This charm is meant to live in your bedroom to protect you from psychic attacks, stress, and outside forces. Cinquefoil is available at most online herbal shops, but if you can't find it, you can substitute rosemary instead.

MATERIALS

5 tablespoons five-finger grass
1 small white, beige, or black drawstring bag
3 drops rosemary essential oil
1 coin (any denomination, size, or metal)

INSTRUCTIONS

1. Put the five-finger grass into the bag and say aloud or internally: *"Cinquefoil, herb of protection, please grant me Mercury's affection."*
2. Add the rosemary oil to the bag and say into the bag: *"I add the magic of rosemary. May this herb protect my home and me."*
3. Add the coin to the bag and say: *"Mercury, please protect this space. I offer this coin in exchange for your presence in this place."*
4. Close the bag and secure it with five knots.
5. Hang the bag in your bedroom above your bed.

BETTER BACK OFF

The color black is associated with protection, warding, and banishing in witchcraft. This charm calls on some of the most powerful botanicals and minerals to help ward off and banish toxic people, enemies, ill-intentioned strangers, and anyone else who might wish to cause you or your household harm. It also encourages those you don't want hanging around your home to leave just as soon as they arrive. Have this charm handy whenever there are unexpected guests, toxic in-laws, or obnoxious people you may want to remove from the premises. Hide the charm wherever you feel the guest will linger the longest.

MATERIALS

5 teaspoons black cohosh
5 black whole peppercorns
1 piece black tourmaline
1 piece obsidian
1 black drawstring bag

INSTRUCTIONS

1. Place the cohosh, peppercorns, tourmaline, and obsidian in the bag.
2. Pull the bag closed and secure it shut by tying five knots.
3. Hold the bag between both hands and close your eyes.
4. As you do, say aloud: *"Black as night, black as stone, protect this space and my home. Banish those who bark and scoff, those who are toxic better back off."*
5. Hide the charm in cushions, under the couch, taped under a table, or anywhere unwanted guests and people may linger.

CIRCLE OF SALT

This is probably the simplest home protection ritual of all. The ritual employs two of the most magical tools in witchcraft: salt and the broom. Perform this ritual prior to spellwork or any other rituals, as this is intended to create a circle of protection, blocking negative outside forces and absorbing spiritual debris so that you are protected within the circle.

MATERIALS

½ cup salt

Small bowl

Broom

INSTRUCTIONS

1. Pour the salt into the bowl.
2. Hold the bowl of salt in your right hand, and use your left hand to sprinkle a circle of salt around you.
3. Allow yourself enough space to move around within the circle.
4. Perform any spell or ritual you wish while inside the circle.
5. With your broom, sweep the salt away to different corners of your space once you've finished your spell or ritual.

VESTA'S SACRED HEARTH FIRE PROTECTION SPELL

The ancient Roman goddess Vesta was integral to ancient Rome. Her sacred flame was kept burning continuously to appease the goddess and secure her protection of the city. We see this history continue today in the act of burning vigil or novena candles. This ritual is meant to replicate the act of an eternal flame, and once lit, the candle should not be extinguished until it goes out on its own.

MATERIALS

1 red permanent marker
1 yellow glass novena/ seven-day candle
Pinch dried angelica (herb)
Pinch salt
Lighter or matches

INSTRUCTIONS

1. Use the permanent marker to write the name "Vesta" on the candle.
2. Hold the candle in both your hands, close your eyes, and ask the goddess internally or aloud to protect your home and sacred space. You may say: *"Goddess Vesta, please protect this place. For you I light this candle in my sacred space."*
3. Sprinkle the angelica and salt on top of the candle.
4. Place the candle in an area where it won't be disturbed and the flame can be contained, such as in a sink.
5. Light the wick, and as the flames burn, reinforce your desire for protection by imagining the flame emitting an aura of protection that envelops the entire home.
6. Keep the candle lit and check on it periodically.
7. When the candle burns out completely, thank Vesta for her protection and patronage, and recycle the glass.

TOIL AND TROUBLE CAULDRON PROTECTION SPELL

You've probably heard the term "fighting fire with fire." This spell does exactly that! Let's face it, no matter how hard we try to avoid negativity, we sometimes end up in the company of toxic people. And if they're in your home, their energy can linger and find its way into your sacred space. This spell uses some of the most powerful protection botanicals, as well as the cleansing properties of Florida water and the transformative and mighty power of fire, to blast away any negativity that may be lingering around your space. Be mindful that this spell is potent and may deliver a karmic whooping to those who deserve it. Perform this spell on a Monday or Saturday evening in the living room or kitchen, where you have space and will be undisturbed.

MATERIALS

- Medium cast-iron cauldron (try to avoid substitutions for this item, but a metal pot may suffice if absolutely necessary)
- 3 pinches salt
- 3 tablespoons Florida water
- Matches
- 3 pinches angelica
- 3 whole bay leaves
- 3 whole juniper berries
- 3 pinches mugwort
- Mortar and pestle

INSTRUCTIONS

1. Place the cauldron on a table or counter in the living room or kitchen.
2. Place both hands over the cauldron, close your eyes, and say: *"Sacred cauldron, fulfill my desire. Banish and purge all toxicity with your enchanted fire."*
3. Put the salt into the cauldron.

4. Pour the Florida water into the cauldron, making sure it saturates the salt.
5. Strike a match and toss it into the cauldron. Keep your face away from the cauldron and be mindful, as Florida water contains alcohol, which can cause the flame to ignite in the cauldron and create a contained fire.
6. One by one, toss in the angelica, bay leaves, juniper berries, and mugwort.
7. Say aloud or internally once all the herbs have been tossed into the cauldron: *"I burn away all toil and trouble and ask for protection, making it double."*
8. Strike one more match and toss it into the cauldron, then say: *"The home of this witch has no room for a bitch. I purge your anger and am protected from danger."*
9. Allow all the flames to go out, and wait for the cauldron and its contents to cool before touching it.
10. Once cooled, take the remaining debris and burned herbs from the cauldron and grind them down into a powderlike substance with the mortar and pestle.
11. Sprinkle the powder outside, along the entryway, and around the perimeter of your home, creating a protective barrier.

HECATE PROTECTION ALTAR

Hecate is the primordial Greco-Roman goddess of witchcraft, necromancy, and the moon. However, she also has a long history as a home and hearth goddess, and she was often petitioned in peoples' homes for protection. Erecting a small altar and inviting Hecate into your home ensures you will be protected and guarded by one of the best-known goddesses of witchcraft. Prepare this altar on the last day of any month or on a Monday. Be sure to tend to it at least once a month with new offerings. This altar will offer continuous protection as long as it is standing and regular offerings are made.

MATERIALS

Cloth or rag (for cleaning)
Black cloth (large enough to cover desired altar space)
Image of Hecate (statue, picture, drawing, or printout)
Lighter or matches
1 stick frankincense incense
Incense holder
3 garlic bulbs
3 whole bay leaves
2 small bowls, preferably white or black
1 black permanent marker
1 white glass novena/seven-day candle
3 pinches wormwood
1 cup water
1 tablespoon olive oil
Candle snuffer

INSTRUCTIONS

1. Find the area or corner you wish to dedicate as Hecate's altar. This can be on top of a dresser, bookshelf, tabletop, or mantel of a fireplace. Create a portable altar with a square wooden box.
2. Wipe down the surface of your altar area with a cloth or rag, and then place the black cloth over it.
3. Place the image of Hecate in the back center of the altar and say: *"Hecate, primordial goddess, I invite you into this sacred space. May you guard and protect my home and place."*

4. Light the stick of frankincense incense and wave it around your space saying: *"Hecate, goddess of witchcraft and sorcery, I dedicate this sacred altar to thee."*
5. Place the incense stick in the incense holder and place both on the altar.
6. Add the garlic bulbs and bay leaves to one of the small bowls.
7. Place the bowl to the left of the image of Hecate and say: *"Oh great goddess of the ancient way, with these offerings I beseech you to stay."*
8. Use the permanent marker to write the name "Hecate" on the candle.
9. Sprinkle the wormwood on the candle and light the wick.
10. Place the candle on the right side of the image of Hecate and say: *"Goddess of witches, I light this sacred flame. Let it burn like a torch in your very name."*
11. Pour water into the other small bowl. Add the olive oil, and using your finger, stir the contents of the bowl together. Sprinkle a bit of the liquid over the altar and say: *"This space is dedicated to mighty Hecate. May she protect me and this space."*
12. Allow the incense to burn down completely.
13. Snuff the candle out, thanking the goddess for her services as you do so.
14. Relight the candle the next day and allow it to burn until it burns down completely, only snuffing the candle if you must leave the home.
15. Toss out the water and oil mixture after three days and replace it with regular water. You may perform additional rituals and spells for Hecate on this altar.

PROTÉGER MA MAISON (PROTECT MY HOME) FLOOR WASH

This recipe is French Creole and was first recorded in a women's folk magic pamphlet. It derives from the book *The Black Folder: Personal Communications on the Mastery of Hoodoo* by Catherine Yronwode. This remedy is most effective when performed during a new moon, the summer solstice, Midsummer's Eve, or Hallows' Eve.

MATERIALS

1 gallon hot water
Large bucket
3 pinches salt
3 pinches vervain
Pinch St. John's wort
1 cup white vinegar
2 cups Florida water
Cloth, rag, or towel
Mop

INSTRUCTIONS

1. Pour the hot water into the bucket.
2. Add the salt, vervain, and St. John's wort to the water.
3. Pour in the vinegar and Florida water.
4. Dip the cloth into the bucket of floor wash and wipe down your windows and other surfaces.
5. Dip the mop in the bucket and clean the floors.
6. Once you've washed the floor and wiped down the surfaces of your home, toss the water in your backyard or down the toilet.
7. Rinse the mop, cloth, and bucket in the sink.

NAILS OF IRON PROTECTION CHARMS

Iron provides protection without the need for it to be charmed or enchanted. It is actually used to counter malevolent witchcraft, as well as protect against faeries, goblins, ghosts, and many other supernatural creatures. Aside from providing protection, iron also enhances spellwork and magic, allowing you to siphon its energy and offering you strength. These charms are meant to be hung above the entryway of your home and above your bed for spiritual protection. If you need to be discreet, the charms can be hidden in a potted plant by the door or under a floor mat.

MATERIALS

4 medium iron nails, grouped in pairs

Scissors

Red or black string (thick) or twine

INSTRUCTIONS

1. Arrange each pair of nails into the shape of an equal-armed cross.
2. Use the scissors to cut a 12-inch length of string. Wrap the string around the middle of the first set of nails, securing them into the desired shape.
3. Tie and knot the string, allowing enough string to tie it again and make a loop to hang.
4. Repeat steps 2 and 3 for the second set of nails.
5. Hang one crossed-nail charm above the entryway of your home.
6. Hang the second crossed-nail charm above your bed.

24/7 PROTECTION POTION

Apollo is the Greco-Roman god of light and prophecy, and Diana, his twin sister, is the goddess of night and magic. Their associated herbs are St. John's wort (Apollo) and mugwort (Diana), two powerful botanicals with intense protective qualities. This potion attracts spirit allies to protect you and your home as well as to enhance your magical and intuitive powers. It acts as both a wash and tea. Create this brew and drink one cup at the beginning of the day and a cup before you go to bed.

MATERIALS

Teapot or heat-safe pot
2 cups water
1 tablespoon St. John's wort
1 tablespoon mugwort
Heat-safe mug
Sugar, honey, and/or milk (optional)
Mason jar or glass with lid
Paper towels

INSTRUCTIONS

1. Using a teapot or heat-safe pot, heat the water on your stove for several minutes at the start of your day. Do not bring to a boil.
2. Add the St. John's wort and mugwort to the water.
3. Allow the mixture to simmer for several minutes.
4. Pour about one cup of the mixture into the mug.
5. Sweeten your potion as desired with sugar, cream, milk, or honey (if using).
6. Hold your mug in both hands, close your eyes, and say: *"Lord Apollo, god of light, protect my day and make it bright."*
7. Drink as much of the brew from your mug as you can, and pour the rest into the sink.
8. Save the mixture that remains in the pot for the evening.

9. Reheat your mixture in the stove or microwave at bedtime.
10. Pour your brew into a mug and sweeten it as desired.
11. Hold the mug in both hands, close your eyes, and say: *"Dear Diana, queen of witches and goddess of night, protect my slumber and my household until noon."*
12. Drink as much of the mixture from the mug as you can, and pour the rest into the sink.
13. Save any remaining mixture from your pot and pour it into a mason jar. Secure the lid and keep it in a cupboard or dark space.
14. Dip paper towels into the mixture the following morning, and wipe down the kitchen counter, windows, doorway frames, and hard surfaces of your bedroom with them.
15. As you do, say, *"Apollo and Diana, celestial and divine, protect this space, and all that is mine."*
16. Pour the remaining contents down the sink or into the toilet and flush it.

SATOR SQUARE OF PROTECTION

This simple charm packs quite a punch. Dating back to ancient Rome, around 79 CE, this mysterious Latin palindrome is linked to Christian, Jewish, and pagan protection magic. It was carved and etched into many homes, temples, and sacred sites throughout Italy and other parts of Europe. This charm is so powerful that malevolent forces, demons, and those with ill intent are reputed to be unable to stay in the same room as this magic square.

MATERIALS

- 1 red pen
- 1 square piece of unlined paper (at least 2 x 2 inches)
- 1 piece clear tape
- 1 piece white chalk (optional)

INSTRUCTIONS

1. Use the red pen to write this charm on the square piece of paper:
    - S A T O R
    - A R E P O
    - T E N E T
    - O P E R A
    - R O T A S
2. Tape the square prominently or discreetly in the room or space you wish to protect.
3. Optionally, draw this charm with white chalk outside your home or on your block to protect the area where you live.

WITCH'S PROTECTION BOTTLE

Witch bottles have been used throughout Europe and colonial America to protect homes against, well, witches. Now witches have reclaimed this magic to protect their own homes from unwanted guests, both physical and supernatural. This simple spell bottle is a staple in witchcraft and folk magic. *Be sure the jar's mouth is big enough that you can put your hand inside.*

MATERIALS

3 sewing pins
3 sewing needles
3 small iron nails
1 small or medium mason jar with lid
3 pinches salt
3 pinches black pepper
Lighter or matches
1 white or black chime candle

INSTRUCTIONS

1. Place the pins, needles, and nails inside the mason jar with the pointed ends facing upward.
2. Spit into the bottle and say aloud: *"By my witch's spit, I invoke this charm. Protect my hearth and house from harm."*
3. Add the salt to the jar, followed by the pepper.
4. Secure the top of the jar and then light the chime candle, placing it on top of the jar and allowing the wax to drip and melt over the top.
5. Say: *"I invoke the household guardians to protect this space and me. By the sealing of this bottle as I will it, so mote it be."*
6. Blow out the candle, and allow the wax on the jar to cool.
7. Bury the jar in front of your home.

of FORTUNE

CHAPTER 7

Energizing the Home

After a long day, sometimes nothing feels better than plopping down on the sofa or bed and conking out. Sometimes, you may feel this way even if you haven't left the house all day. Being spiritually connected all the time can leave you feeling lethargic and drained. Instead of turning to coffee or an energy drink for a boost, let it be your home that energizes you. When your home is energized, you can siphon that energy and use it to boost your spirits. In this chapter, we will cover some basic spells and charms to energize your home, so that when you hit a low, you can turn to your home for that magical zap you need.

ASHES TO ASHES PHOENIX POWDER

The phoenix is a mythological creature said to have regenerative powers. Once the phoenix reached the end of its life, it would perish in a burst of flames, only to come back from the ashes renewed. This powder helps you feel renewed and refreshed, like a phoenix emerging from its own ashes. The key ingredient? Leftover ash or debris from previous spellwork. Make this powder during a dark moon or on a Sunday, and sprinkle it in the corners of your bedroom.

MATERIALS

Ash or debris from previous spellwork
Cauldron
3 pinches salt
3 tablespoons Florida water
Matches
3 pinches myrrh
3 pinches frankincense
Mortar and pestle
Mason jar

INSTRUCTIONS

1. Place the ash and previous spellwork leftovers in the cauldron.
2. Add the salt to the cauldron and sprinkle in the Florida water.
3. Strike a match and toss it into the cauldron.
4. Toss in the myrrh and frankincense while the fire burns.
5. Say aloud: *"Ashes to ashes, dust to dust, the phoenix will rise, this is a must. Energize my sacred space, and let me feel lifted in my space."*
6. Strike another match and toss it into the cauldron.

7. Allow the flames to extinguish completely and the cauldron and its contents to cool.
8. Transfer the contents to the mortar and use the pestle to grind the ingredients into a fine powder.
9. Sprinkle the powder on the four corners of your bedroom and say: *"Energize this space, energize this place. As I will, so mote it be."*
10. Store the remaining powder in a mason jar; you can sprinkle this powder in other areas of the home as well.

MAGICAL MATCHBOX BATTERY CHARM

This charm acts as a battery to energize the home, as well as to neutralize negative residual energy that may be lingering. The herbs and ingredients required to create the charm can be used individually to enhance your energy and personal magic. Make this charm on a full moon or Monday afternoon for maximum effect.

MATERIALS

1 small clear quartz crystal
Empty matchbox
1 tablespoon dragon's blood resin
1 tablespoon sugar
1 tablespoon salt
1 12-inch section red twine

INSTRUCTIONS

1. Place the quartz in the matchbox.
2. Sprinkle the dragon's blood, sugar, and salt over the crystal.
3. Place both your hands over the crystal, close your eyes, and visualize blue light emanating from your hands and onto the crystal, while saying: *"I create this charm to energize my space, to keep me lifted and to energize this place."*
4. Close the matchbox and secure it by wrapping the red twine around it, leaving enough length to knot it closed.
5. Hide the matchbox in the back of a cupboard or drawer.
6. Bury and replace the matchbox once a year or whenever you feel the magic has worn off.

WITCH'S LITTLE BOTTLE OF ENERGY

This charm also serves as a magical battery booster, while promoting happiness and financial success. Make this on a Wednesday and keep it somewhere in the kitchen to enhance the energies of that space.

MATERIALS

1 small citrine crystal
1 small glass vial or bottle with cork lid
1 teaspoon rosemary
1 teaspoon sugar
3 whole coffee beans
Lighter or matches
1 yellow chime candle

INSTRUCTIONS

1. Hold the citrine in your left hand, squeeze your hand into a fist, and say: *"Citrine crystal charge my space, boost the energy of my sacred space."*
2. Place the citrine in the vial and then add the rosemary and sugar.
3. Hold the coffee beans in your left hand, squeeze your hand into a fist, and say: *"Give me strength, give me energy. As I will, so mote it be."*
4. Add the coffee beans to the vial and close it with the cork.
5. Light the chime candle and tilt it over the bottle, allowing the melting wax to drip over the cork.
6. Turn the bottle slowly to make sure the wax drips along all sides of the top, covering and sealing the bottle.
7. Blow out the chime candle and allow the wax to cool and dry, making sure the bottle is fully sealed.
8. Place the bottle in the kitchen and let it do its magic.

FAERY BOREDOM BANISHMENT BAG

Faeries are anything but boring. In fact, they can be quite mischievous and enjoy playing games with us human folk. When things feel stagnant or boring or you have the blues, invite the fae into your life for a little uplifting enchantment. Be mindful, though: Faeries can be quite rambunctious and bring a lot of energy. If it's energy you want, with this charm, it's energy you'll get.

MATERIALS

1 tablespoon angelica
1 tablespoon lavender
1 tablespoon rosebuds or petals
1 small drawstring bag, preferably purple or blue
1 small bell ball (available at any craft or fabric shop)

INSTRUCTIONS

1. Place the herbs in the bag and say: *"I call on the fae, those far and wide, and offer my home for you to reside."*
2. Ring the bell ball several times, then say: *"I ask for your presence to lift the energy of my place, and bring your cheer to my sacred space."*
3. Drop the bell into the bag, pull the drawstring closed, and secure it with three knots.
4. Hang the charm near a window or fireplace to attract the faeries.

HOUSEHOLD SPIRITS ENERGY BREW

The brew is intended to feed the house and the spirits who dwell within it. It can help attract the spirits of your home and geographic areas. And it raises the vibrations of your household. Prepare this brew on a Monday evening for the best results.

MATERIALS

2 cups water
Medium pot
3 tablespoons cinnamon
3 tablespoons nutmeg
3 whole pieces of clove
1 tablespoon mugwort
Mug

INSTRUCTIONS

1. Pour the water into the pot and heat it on the stove.
2. Add the cinnamon, nutmeg, clove, and mugwort.
3. Allow the aroma and steam to fill the kitchen, making sure not to let the brew boil over.
4. Stand over the brew as you say: *"Spirits of earth, and beyond the veil, if you're kind, I invite you from wherever you hail. I brew this offering in my sacred space, so that you can enjoy it in this place."*
5. Remove the pot from the stove and allow the brew to cool.
6. Pour the concoction into a mug and offer it to the spirits by placing it on your altar or the center of the kitchen counter.
7. Pour the rest of the brew over the entryway of your home and in your backyard. If this isn't possible, flush the remaining liquid down the toilet.
8. Allow the mug to sit with the brew for three days. After that, thank the spirits and pour out the brew, either out the front or back entryway of your home or down the sink.

ENERGIZER BUNNY BUDDY

Despite their adorable appearance, rabbits and hares have a strong association with witchcraft and the occult. They are said to be the familiars and sacred animals of various pagan goddesses, such as Cerridwen, Freya, Diana/Artemis, Holda, and Eostre. Rabbits and hares tend to dwell within the realms of the supernatural, and they were known to be able to jump between worlds. While thought to be nocturnal creatures, they have been known to dart about at all hours of the day, especially during mating season. This plush bunny totem is enchanted to give you energy whenever you need it. If you feel sad or blue, give it a squeeze to have it help you.

MATERIALS

- Rabbit plush stuffed animal or soft toy
- 3 drops orange essential oil
- 3 drops lavender essential oil
- 3 drops cinnamon essential oil

INSTRUCTIONS

1. Hold the rabbit and give it a hug, closing your eyes and saying: *"Swift spirit of rabbit, energize my home. This space is yours, you're free to roam."*
2. Add the essential oils to different parts of the plush toy (e.g., orange to the ears, lavender to the belly, and cinnamon to the feet).
3. Say: *"The hare and rabbit energize my space, and their spirits reside within this place."*
4. Name your rabbit and hold or place it close to you when you need energy.

ENCHANTED ENERGY MIST

Citrus is known to enhance energy and provide a little magically cheerful boost. This wonderful spray is a perfect way to neutralize any stagnant energy in the home and make your sacred space more uplifting and psychically charged. Spritz this mist around the home whenever you feel it needs a little oomph.

MATERIALS

Medium-size spray bottle
1½ cups water
6 drops lemon essential oil
4 drops citronella essential oil
2 drops vetiver essential oil

INSTRUCTIONS

1. Fill the spray bottle with the water, making sure to leave enough room for the essential oils.
2. Add the essential oils to the water in the bottle.
3. Screw on the bottle cap and shake the bottle vigorously to mix the oils and water.
4. Spray your mist around the home, in corners and entryways to enhance the energy of the space.
5. Keep your bottle stored in a cool, dark place and use as needed.

TIGER'S EYE ENERGY CHARM

Tiger's eye is a wonderful stone with many magical properties. However, it is mostly known for its association with courage, protection, and stamina. This charm is perfect to have on your desk when you need to focus or work on a task or project. Need the energy to finish schoolwork, write an email, or finish a task? Let this bit of magic assist you.

MATERIALS

- 1 5 x 5-inch square orange fabric
- 3 pieces tumbled tiger's eye
- 3 pinches salt
- 3 pinches rosemary
- 1 10-inch section black string or thread

INSTRUCTIONS

1. Lay out the orange fabric in the center of your work space and place the three pieces of tiger's eye in the middle of the square.
2. Sprinkle the salt and rosemary on top of the stones.
3. Pull up the corner of the fabric, pinching the ends together and twisting the fabric to form a ball, and secure the stones and herbs.
4. Wrap the string several times around the bunched-up fabric, preventing the stones from moving, and tie three knots.
5. Hold the charm between both your hands, close your eyes, and say: *"May this charm energize my space and those who reside within this space."*
6. Place the charm by your computer, near your desk, or in your work space to help keep you motivated and focused.

SELENITE CIRCULATION SPELL

Selenite is a salt-based crystal that is known to charge other crystals and ritual tools. Use this spell any time you want to energize and uplift the space around you. Perform this spell on a Saturday or Monday afternoon to achieve the best results.

MATERIALS

1 stick selenite
1 small crystal quartz
Pinch rosemary

INSTRUCTIONS

1. Place the selenite stick by a window.
2. Clutch the quartz in your hand, close your eyes, and say: *"Energize my sacred space. Lift the spirits of this place."*
3. Place the quartz on top of the selenite stick.
4. Sprinkle the rosemary on the stones and say, *"By my magic, I enchant those stones to energize my home and its bones."*
5. Leave the crystals by the window until the next full moon, then gift them to someone who may need to energize their home.

MIGHTY MITHRAS MOTIVATION RITUAL

We all have those days when although we know we have obligations waiting for us, such as work or class, we simply aren't feeling it. Mithras is a Greco-Roman solar deity associated with courage, light, joy, and strength. This spell is the perfect way to perk yourself up and plunge into your day. It will energize not only you but your home as well. Feel free to perform this fun ritual as often as you like, preferably in the morning when you wake up, but make sure you give yourself adequate time for it in the morning.

MATERIALS

- Lighter or matches
- 1 stick frankincense
- Incense holder
- 1 cup preferred caffeinated beverage (e.g., coffee or tea) or orange juice if you don't drink caffeine
- Your favorite mug
- Playlist
- Speakers or headphones

INSTRUCTIONS

1. Take a few deep breaths while you're still in bed, then begin to stretch.
2. Say, while still in bed: *"Mighty Mithras, god of light, give me energy and strength to burn true and bright."*
3. Light the stick of frankincense and place it in the incense holder.
4. Prepare yourself a cup of tea, coffee, or orange juice in your favorite mug.
5. Play your favorite high-energy song that brings you joy and makes you want to sing and dance.

6. Begin to move a little as the music plays, feeling yourself give in to the beat of the music. Imagine that you're at a club or party as you let your body flow.
7. Absorb the energy of the music and send it into your space, touching the walls, doors, and surfaces around you.
8. Head back to your bed, lie on it, and say: *"Mighty Mithras, energize my space. Let me feel motivated in this space."*
9. Continue with the rest of your preparations for the day.

MAENAD MADNESS ENERGY SPELL

Maenads are the female followers of the Greek god of wine, theater, and revelry, Dionysus, also known as Bacchus to the Romans. They were known to lead ecstatic rituals and stir people into a frenzy. This spell is derived from an ancient Greek ritual meant to enhance and maintain energy in a sacred space. Perform this spell during midsummer or on a Friday or Saturday evening when you're alone and have privacy.

MATERIALS

Lighter or matches
1 stick frankincense
Incense holder
3 tablespoons rose petals
3 purple grapes
3 gold-colored coins (plastic or chocolate coins are suitable)
1 purple drawstring bag
3 drops olive oil

INSTRUCTIONS

1. Light the frankincense and place it in the holder.
2. Use your hands to waft the incense smoke toward you, as if bathing yourself in the smoke, and say: *"Dionysus, godly and divine, energize this space, both yours and mine."*
3. Place the rose petals, grapes, and coins in the purple bag.
4. Add the three drops of olive oil to the bag and say: *"Energy is what I shall reclaim. I make this charm in Bacchus's name."*
5. Tie the bag closed and secure it with three knots.
6. Hold the bag in your left hand as you dance and skip around your entire home, chanting: *"Io, Io, Dionysus, Io, Io, Bacchus."*
7. Envision your home getting energized, and touch the walls and surfaces as you chant, dance, and skip.

8. Repeat step 6 at least three times throughout the entire space.
9. Bury the charm bag in the front of your home, or hide it in a potted plant or bush.
10. Thank Dionysus.

WHEEL OF FORTUNE ENERGY SPELL

The Wheel of Fortune in tarot is a card of cycles, new beginnings, destiny, and luck. This spell harnesses the archetypal aspects of the tarot and uses it to energize your sacred space, reminding you that luck is on your side and that there's no need to stress, by creating a simple altar.

MATERIALS

Wheel of Fortune tarot card
3 pieces of clear quartz
1 piece selenite

INSTRUCTIONS

1. Find a flat surface that you wish to use as a temporary altar.
2. Place the Wheel of Fortune card in the center of that surface.
3. Arrange two of the quartz pieces on both sides of the card and the third on top.
4. Place the piece of selenite under the card.
5. Hold both hands over the center of the card, close your eyes, and say: *"Wheel of Fortune, mighty and great, spin for me and wield my fate. Let me feel energized before it's too late."*
6. Repeat step 5 every day for seven days.

CHAPTER 8

Blessing the Home

I think of a blessing like the bestowing of a magical kiss, favor, or reward. When you bless your home, you are charging it with magic and reinforcing its spiritual power. A blessing can be as simple or complex as you like. Blessings can be done through prayer or speaking magical words, making amulets or talismans, or working a ritual. Blessing a home through witchcraft is more ritualistic, usually calling on spirit aids or deities to assist in the blessing. Magical house blessings through witchcraft are actually very similar to blessings you'd find in Catholicism, Judaism, Hinduism, Islam, and other religions.

BRIGHT BRIGID BLESSING

The Celtic goddess Brigid is a wonderful deity to invoke for house blessings. She is the goddess of the hearth, after all. Perform this house blessing in your kitchen, as it's the room where she'd feel most at home. Consider sitting in meditation after performing this blessing to feel how the vibration of your home may be changed as a result of this act.

MATERIALS

1 white chime candle
1 drop olive oil
1 chime candleholder
Lighter or matches
Water
Small bowl
Pinch salt
1 sprig fresh rosemary

INSTRUCTIONS

1. Anoint the white candle with the olive oil, and as you rub oil on the candle, say: *"I anoint this candle with sacred oil in hopes to wipe away pain and toil."*
2. Place the candle in the holder and light the wick. When the candle is lit, say: *"Great goddess Brigid of the mighty hearth, bless my home with peace, love, and mirth."*
3. Put enough water into the bowl to nearly fill it.
4. Sprinkle the salt into the water.
5. Dip the sprig of rosemary into the water.
6. Use the wet sprig to fling the water around your kitchen, directing the water toward the corners of the room while saying: *"Brigid, bless my sacred space, as I invite you to this place."*
7. Allow the chime candle to burn down completely.
8. Pour out the water in your backyard, or if that's not feasible, flush it down the toilet.
9. Save the rosemary and allow it to dry out to use in spellwork that requires rosemary.

BESOM (BROOM) BLESSING

The witch's broom, or besom, as it is known in Wicca, has a long history of being used in house blessings and is often the primary tool used to cleanse and bless sacred space in folk magic around the world. This broom blessing can be done whenever you wish to uplift the vibrations of your sacred space spiritually and magically. This is a particularly useful blessing if family members or friends have recently come through your space, as sometimes visitors leave behind traces of their own energy, which may or may not be aligned with the energy of your home.

MATERIALS

Broom
Pinch vervain
Pinch salt
1 tablespoon Florida water

INSTRUCTIONS

1. Hold the broom vertically in both hands and say: *"Witch's broom I consecrate thee. Bless my home and those around me."*
2. Hold the broom with the bristles facing upward and sprinkle the vervain and salt on top of the bristles.
3. Say: *"Bless my space and bless my home, and discourage bad entities who wander and roam."*
4. Sprinkle the Florida water over the bristles and say: *"This besom is charged to bless my space. Any unwanted energies it shall erase."*
5. Prop the broom by the entryway of your home or by the window closest to your entrance. If discretion is needed, place it bristles up in the closet nearest to the entryway.

ANCIENT OG HOUSE BLESSING

Frankincense and myrrh are more than just gifts the Three Kings bestowed upon the baby Jesus. They are tried-and-true magical resins that have been used to bless and purify sacred space for many millennia. The ancient Egyptians, Greeks, and Romans used this enchanted blend as an offering to deities and spirits alike. Burn this incense blend whenever you wish to petition deities, bless your space, or provide an offering to the spirit realm.

MATERIALS

1 charcoal disk
Lighter or matches
Heat-safe dish metal or ceramic (avoid glass)
1 teaspoon frankincense resin
1 teaspoon myrrh resin

INSTRUCTIONS

1. Light the charcoal disk and place it on the heat-safe dish. When the disk begins to spark and turn gray, sprinkle the frankincense and myrrh on the charcoal.
2. Hold the dish in your right hand and walk around your space, wafting the smoke in different areas of your space with your left hand.
3. As you do this, chant, "*I bless my home with ancient ways. Spirits and deities, protect me with your mighty gaze.*"
4. Allow the incense to burn down completely. Flush the remaining charcoal debris.

HAPPY HOME RITUAL BLESSING

This ritual uses the symbol of the equal-armed cross and the renewing properties of water to bless your space and attract happiness. While the ritual requires only water, salt, and your words, you may wish to burn some incense, such as frankincense, to enhance its potency.

MATERIALS

Pinch salt

1 wineglass filled with water

INSTRUCTIONS

1. Sprinkle the salt into the glass or goblet filled with water and say: *"By the powers of water and earth, bless this space with happiness and mirth."*
2. Dip your index finder in the water and draw an equal-armed cross (+) on all the walls and surfaces in your home.
3. Sprinkle some or all of the remaining water around your home with your fingers.
4. Leave the glass and whatever water may be left in it on your altar or by a window for twenty-four hours to purify and bless your space. After twenty-four hours, pour the water down the sink or flush it.

TRIPLE FAERY HOUSE BLESSING

Just like in the Walt Disney classic *Sleeping Beauty*, faeries can be benevolent, bestowing blessings upon us, while also being notorious tricksters. This house blessing petitions the legendary fae in hopes of getting them on our side. Perform this spell any day of the week during an even hour (e.g., 6, 8, 10, or 12 a.m. or p.m.) or during the summer or winter equinox.

MATERIALS

Lighter or matches
1 blue chime candle
Small round dish
Pinch mugwort
Pinch lavender
Pinch rosebuds
Bell
3 coins (any size or denomination)

INSTRUCTIONS

1. Light the bottom of the chime candle a bit and secure the base to the dish so that it stands upright.
2. Sprinkle the mugwort on the dish in a circle around the candle and say: *"Mighty mugwort, herb of the spirit world, invite the fae into this place, so that they may bless my space."*
3. Sprinkle the lavender in a circle around the candle and say: *"Lavender, with scent divine, attract the fae into this space of mine."*
4. Sprinkle the rosebuds in a circle around the candle and say: *"Roses that bloomed through summer and spring, call forth the faeries in this sacred ring."*
5. Light the candle, and as the flame burns, say: *"Faeries gather in this ring. Please be present at this house blessing."*
6. Ring the bell three times and say: *"I invite the supernatural elements and benevolent spirits to bless this space."*

7. Allow the candle to burn down completely. When the candle has extinguished, place the three coins on the dish within the rings of herbs and say: *"I leave these coins as payment in kind, for blessing my home and paying me mind."*
8. Allow the dish to remain out for an entire day, and on the following evening, dispose of the herbs by tossing them out your front door or flushing them.

BRIGHT LEMON BLESSINGS

Citrus fruits like lemons are wonderful for house blessings and cleansings, as citrus not only absorbs negative energy, but it also attracts benevolent spirits. Perform this house blessing in the morning with the windows open and lights on to infuse the house with solar energy and eradicate stagnant vibrations that might be lingering about.

MATERIALS

3 lemons

Knife

INSTRUCTIONS

1. Open all the blinds or drapes in your home to let in as much natural light as possible. If you don't have that many windows, turn on all the lights in your home.
2. Cut the lemons in half with the knife and say: *"Sacred citrus, bless my space and invite happiness to this witch's place."*
3. Place the lemon halves in different corners of your home. Allow the lemon halves to sit there for three consecutive days to bless your home.
4. After three days, collect the lemon halves and bury them in your backyard or in a potted plant.

YE OLDE HOUSE WITCH'S BLESSING OIL

This eighteenth-century recipe is perfect for blessing your home, as well as your sacred tools and other magical objects. Its origins are from Wales in the United Kingdom. Just dab a bit onto your finger and mark the walls, windows, and other surfaces of your home with an X or equal-armed cross (+). Make this oil during a full moon for a more magical boost. Store it in an amber-colored bottle so the mixture isn't degraded by ultraviolet rays.

MATERIALS

3 whole cloves
1 2-ounce amber bottle
1½ ounces olive oil
3 drops rosemary oil
3 drops rose oil
2 drops lemon oil

INSTRUCTIONS

1. Put the cloves into the bottle.
2. Pour in the olive oil.
3. Add the essential oils, seal the bottle, and shake it while saying: *"This witch's oil will bless my space and the sacred tools in this place."*
4. Dab a bit of the blessing oil on your index finger and anoint the walls, windows, and surfaces with the oil by drawing an X or +.
5. Seal the bottle and store in a cool, dark place.

"RUE FOR YOU" BLESSING RITUAL

These famous words were spoken by Ophelia in Shakespeare's *Hamlet* as she gifted the queen a bundle of rue as an offering of forgiveness. Rue is quite a potent magical botanical that is often linked to protection. It was known to ward off the evil eye, as well as witches, demons, and other supernatural creatures. Eventually, it made its way into the Catholic Church, where it was used as an active ingredient in exorcisms. Today, rue is known as the herb of grace and is useful in spells for cleansing, healing, and blessing. This ritual is comprised of several steps and may take a little over a week to finish, but it packs a mighty punch in the realm of blessings. Fresh rue can be acquired at most specialty food markets or Hispanic markets or from any online apothecary.

MATERIALS

- 1 fresh bundle of rue
- 1 6-inch section of twine
- Hammer
- 1 nail
- Lighter or matches
- 1 blue glass-encased seven-day/novena candle
- Candle snuffer (optional)

INSTRUCTIONS

1. Tie the bundle of rue together with the twine, hold it in your hands, and say: *"Spirits dwelling within this space, here I offer the herb of grace. Rue for you, and rue for me, so bless this space I beg of thee."*
2. Hammer the nail above your bed and hang the rue upside down from it.
3. Allow the rue to dry out completely, or let it hang at least for three full nights, before removing the bundle from above your bed.

4. Pick off pieces of the dried rue and grind them between your fingers, sprinkling them over the candle. Do this three times, so that you have about three sprinkles of herbs.
5. Light the wick of the candle and say: *"Herb of grace, bless this place and banish malevolent spirits from this witch's space."*
6. Place the candle in a space such as a bathroom sink or tub, where it will be contained, and allow it to burn down completely, checking on it every so often. Do not blow the candle out, and if you must extinguish it, use a candle snuffer.
7. Thank the spirits of the place once the candle has burned completely out.
8. Place the remaining dried rue into the glass and bury it in your backyard or recycle it to keep the magic moving.

HAPPY HAUNTS BLESSING INCENSE

House witchery requires building a relationship with the spirits of the home, place, and bioregion we reside in. This magical incense is perfect for attracting benevolent spirits and blessing your home with some supernatural assistance. Burn this incense during a full moon, on Halloween, or during midsummer for more potent effects.

MATERIALS

1 tablespoon mugwort
1 tablespoon lavender
1 tablespoon rosemary
2 tablespoons frankincense
Mortar and pestle
Charcoal disk
Heat-safe dish
Lighter or matches
Small glass vial or bottle with cork top or cap

INSTRUCTIONS

1. Place the mugwort, lavender, rosemary, and frankincense into the mortar and use the pestle to grind them, making sure all the ingredients are mixed together and any large pieces are broken and mashed up.
2. Place the charcoal disk in the dish and light it, allowing it to burn for several seconds before sprinkling the powder over the disk.
3. Take the dish in your hands as the incense is burning and walk through the home, wafting the smoke about with your hands.
4. As you do this, say, *"Benevolent spirits of this place, I call you to this sacred space. Haunt this home with happiness and mirth. Bless this home with the powers of spirit and earth."*
5. Bottle up the remaining mixture and save it to use during other rituals when you wish benevolent spirits to be present.

HORSESHOE HOME BLESSING

Ever see a home with a horseshoe nailed above the entryway? This lucky charm dates back one thousand years. According to English legend, a blacksmith who would later become St. Dunstan was approached by the devil, disguised as a traveler, to make shoes for his horse. However, Dunstan saw through the devil's disguise and nailed a horseshoe instead to one of the devil's hooves. The devil begged for Dunstan to remove the horseshoe. Dunstan eventually agreed, but under one condition: that the devil respect the horseshoe and never enter any dwelling or place if one was hung above the door. This charm is not only popular but also simple.

MATERIALS

Pinch salt
Small bowl of water
Horseshoe (you can find them at occult, antique, and equestrian shops, as well as online)
Hammer
3 iron nails

INSTRUCTIONS

1. Sprinkle the salt into the bowl of water and stir the mixture with your finger.
2. Sprinkle the water over the horseshoe and say: *"St. Dunstan, bless this space, and keep the devil out of this place."*
3. Use the hammer and nails to hang the horseshoe above the entryway of your home with the open side facing upward.
4. Sprinkle the remaining water over the entryway of your home and say: *"The horseshoe is hung, the home is blessed. This space is charged with happiness, peace, and rest."*

HEARTH AND HOME BLESSING

We've spoken about the significance of the hearth in traditional magic and how important the home is to any witch, not just as a place of refuge, but also as a place that holds energy you can tap into at will for spellwork. This ritual uses your kitchen as the spiritual hearth and blesses your surrounding home. Begin this blessing during the day for best results.

MATERIALS

1 5 x 5-inch white cloth
Lighter or matches
1 stick frankincense
Incense holder
Pinch salt
Bowl of water
Glass-encased orange candle
Candle snuffer (optional)

INSTRUCTIONS

1. Lay out the white cloth on a counter or other flat surface.
2. Light the frankincense, walk clockwise around the kitchen, and say: *"Hestia, Vesta, and Mighty Hera, I call on you to bless this space."*
3. Place the frankincense in the incense holder and set it on any of the four corners of the white cloth.
4. Sprinkle the salt in the bowl of water.
5. Then walking clockwise around your kitchen, sprinkle the water.
6. As you do this, say: *"Goddesses of the sacred hearth, I bless this space with happiness and mirth."*
7. Place the bowl of water on one of the corners of the white cloth.
8. Place the candle in the center of the cloth and light the wick.

9. As the candle burns, say: *"I call upon the goddesses of hearth and home. May you bless this space and allow only benevolent spirits to roam."*
10. Allow the candle to burn all day, extinguishing it only in the evening with a snuffer (do not blow it out), and say: *"The hearth and home are blessed, thanks to the powers of the goddess."*
11. Clean up and discard any remaining debris or contents. Burn the candle again the following day and for several days, until it burns completely out on its own.

MEDEA'S CAULDRON BLESSING

Medea is one of the greatest witches from antiquity. Her grandfather was Helios, the sun god, and her aunt was the mighty enchantress Circe. She was also a priestess of Hecate, the goddess of witchcraft. Medea was said to have an enchanted cauldron that she used to bless the unlucky, rejuvenate the elderly, and even resurrect the dead. She was knowledgeable in the use of botanicals and baneful poisons, as well as protection magic. This ritual has been modified from Medea's ritual found in Ovid's *Metamorphoses*. Perform this ritual during the evening before bed.

MATERIALS

Pinch salt
Cauldron (any size) filled with water
3 drops olive oil
Pinch mullein
3 garlic cloves
Pinch mugwort
Pinch lavender
Lighter or matches
1 sprig rosemary

INSTRUCTIONS

1. Sprinkle the salt into the cauldron.
2. Hold both of your hands over the cauldron and say: *"Mighty Hecate, whose torches burn bright, I ask for your presence as I perform this ritual tonight."*
3. Add the olive oil to the cauldron and say: *"Sacred cauldron of ancient power, I call forth Medea's secrets during this witching hour."*
4. Add the mullein, garlic, mugwort, and lavender to the cauldron and say: *"Herbs of magic and sorcery, bless this space. So mote it be."*

5. Light the sprig of rosemary, allow it to burn for several seconds, and then plunge it into the cauldron's water, extinguishing the flame.
6. Stir the cauldron with the rosemary sprig and say: *"This space is blessed with sorcery, in the name of Hecate."*
7. Place the cauldron in an area where it can be left undisturbed.
8. Leave the cauldron alone for three nights, and after the third night, pour the contents of the cauldron out over the entryway to your home. If that's not possible, simply flush the contents.

A FINAL WORD

You have taken quite a magical journey, bringing you to the end of this enchanting tome. You are now prepared to conjure up all the magic you need to enchant, cleanse, purify, protect, and bless your witchy home. However, there is still more work to be done.

As you advance in your house witchery practice, you can enhance it by gaining familiarity with botanicals and herbs and their magical properties. Many can be used to cleanse your space, so do this regularly, experimenting with different formulations to see which ones you—and your home—like best. Continue to learn about different house spirits and build a relationship with them, as well as ancestors and deities, to keep leveling up your magical practice.

Research different aspects of folk magic and witchcraft, maybe even delving into your genealogy. What were your ancestors' native customs, and how could they apply to your practice? Additionally, remember that many of the mundane practices associated with maintaining a household are also linked to magic and folklore to keep the vibration of your home high.

As always, it is important to protect your space, as it is a sanctuary in which you can practice and grow your craft. Maintain an altar dedicated to the deities of the hearth, and make offerings to house spirits regularly. You may use divination if the frequency in your home seems off and determine what kind of magic should be employed to bring your space back into balance. Now go forth, grab your broom, and connect with your hearth and home.

NOTES

NOTES

CORRESPONDENCES

CANDLE COLORS

black: Wisdom, death, renewal, and resurrection

blue: Peace and tranquility

brown: The earth, strength, balance, justice, earth magic, animal and pet spells, and nature spirits

gold: Abundance, prosperity, attraction, and money

gray: Knowledge, communication, spirit communication, neutralizing negative energy, and wisdom

green: Luck, prosperity, wealth, fertility, stability, abundance, and success

indigo: Renewal, relaxation, reflection, and new beginnings

orange: Energy, exuberance, courage, the sun, positive outcomes, job successes, and wish fulfillment

pink: Affection, compassion, beauty, fidelity, new love, happiness, romantic relationships, monogamy, and marriage

purple: Royalty, the divine, power, and the supernatural

red: Life force, vitality, attraction, sensuality, desire, ambition, virility, strength, birth, death, achieving goals, overcoming obstacles, and love

silver: Clairvoyance, motherhood, marriage, psychic work, money, financial stability, and peace

white: Life, fertility, nourishment, goodness, balance, death, and structure

yellow: Brilliance, joy, clarity, insight, clairvoyance, unhexing, uncrossing, protection, and guidance

HERBS

allspice: Healing, luck, business attraction, money, and prosperity

angelica root: Joy, happiness, empowerment, spiritual communication, protection, and healing

anise: Psychic development, protection from evil eye, and spirit communication

basil: Happiness, money, confidence, love, and protection

bay laurel: Wishing, success, healing, psychic visions, cleansing, wisdom, and power

catnip: Love, sexuality, peace, and protection of children

cinnamon: Money, protection, energy boost, spirituality boost, success, and libido

cloves: Money, luck, and friendship

damiana: Love, sex, aphrodisiac, lust, passion, romance, and attraction

jasmine: Moon magic, love, feminine energy, spirituality, peace, money, sexuality, and health

lavender: Protection, sleep, happiness, peace, astral projection, meditation, love, and purification

lemongrass: Purification, road opener, home in earth, spirit work, and cleansing

mugwort: Psychic powers, prophetic dreams, astral projection, protection, spirit work, strength, deity work, necromancy, and divination

nutmeg: Luck, energy boost, money, raise vibrations, and increase in psychic awareness

pepper (black/white): Protection, return to sender, grounding, and hex breaker

rose: Love, peace, sex, romance, beauty, and self-esteem

rosemary: Protection, cleansing, love, longevity, health, and magic boost

sage: Calming, longevity, wisdom, relaxation, inspiration, spiritual cleansing, and fumigation

thyme: Luck, dreams, money, financial stability, and peace

valerian root: Love, purification, marriage, return to sender, ritual purification, love, and sleep

vervain: Protection, aphrodisiac, inspiration, protection, hex breaker, and spirit protection

wormwood: Prophecy, psychic development, healing, creativity, love, peace, wisdom, and ancestral magic

yarrow: Love, psychic enhancement, wisdom, courage, depression, mental health, and clarity

OILS

amber: Money, sensuality, goddess energy, psychic powers, ancestral work, and protection

bergamot: Money, happiness, cleansing, and peace

cypress: Healing, comfort, grieving, and longevity

dragon's blood: Magic, power, protection, healing, luck, and spiritual clearing

eucalyptus: Healing, protection, and uncrossing

frankincense: Protection, purification, spirituality, meditation, anxiety, fear, soothing, calmness, and higher consciousness

honeysuckle: Prosperity, psychic awareness, protection, sweetness of life, spiritual insight, and goal fulfillment

jasmine: Confidence, love, sex, money, peace, spirituality, insight, and lunar magic

lotus: Egyptian magic, wisdom, blessings, and goddess magic

musk: Courage, masculine energy, fertility, attraction, lust, and sex magic

myrrh: Protection, purification, meditation, grounding, confidence, spiritual awakening, and spiritual fumigation

olive oil: Purification, cleansing, divine energy, spiritual awakening, spirit work, and ritual purification

orange blossom: Joy, money, happiness, personal development, and banishing negative thoughts

patchouli: Fertility, physical energy, romance, partnership, divine self, attraction, and money

peppermint: Protection, calming, wisdom, spirituality, cleansing, happiness, and positivity stimulant

rose: Beauty, love, sex, peace, psychic protection, and honesty

sandalwood: Wish fulfillment, healing, spirituality, protection, sexual awakening, attraction, and higher consciousness

vanilla: Love, magic, mental awareness, energy, sex, fights depression, and relationships

violet: Love, wish fulfillment, healing, calmness, and peace

ylang-ylang: Aphrodisiac, attraction, euphoria, relaxation, bliss, love, and grounding

DAYS OF THE WEEK

Sunday: "Sun's day," great for manifestation, male energy, divine power, courage, and spells for happiness, success, and job opportunities

Monday: "Moon's day," ruled by the power of the moon and lunar deities, and great for dreamwork, spiritual growth, psychic and divination work, healing, and cleansing

Tuesday: "Mars day," ruled by the planet Mars, the Roman god of war, and perfect for performing spellwork for courage, conflict resolution, virility, gaining wisdom, or overcoming obstacles

Wednesday: "Mercury's day," ruled by the planet Mercury, and the perfect time for spellwork involving self-improvement, communication, divination, travel, friendships, and spirit communication

Thursday: Ruled by the planet Jupiter, this day is great for spells regarding money, legal matters, luck, and success

Friday: Ruled by the planet Venus and the Norse fertility goddess Frigg, this day is great for spellwork and rituals concerning love, friendship, art, creativity, pleasure, and fertility

Saturday: Ruled by the planet Saturn, this day is great for spellwork and rituals concerning banishing, hex breaking, cleansing, healing, returning to sender, and motivation

LUNAR CYCLES

new moon: New beginnings, uncover hidden agendas, uncover the truth, spiritual awakening, cleansing, protection of home and self, and bindings

waxing moon: Money spells, financial stability, job attraction, energy intensity, abundance, and growth

full moon: Healing, wish fulfillment, goddess magic, prosperity, spirit work, love magic, and attraction

waning moon: Banishing, purging, getting rid of negativity, protection, change, letting go

STONES

agate: Health, luck, and gambling

amber: Love, luck, and transformation

amethyst: Fights addiction, psychic awareness, insight, healing, crown chakra, and spirit work

Apache tears: Protection, comfort, ancestral magic, and cleansing

bloodstone: "Stone of courage," purification, clearing negativity, and balance

carnelian: Creation, creativity, life force, fear, stability, virility, and health

citrine: Prosperity, abundance, money, mental focus, and endurance

hematite: Health, grounding, return to sender, relaxation, peace, and spirit work

jet: Protection, earth magic, spirit cleanse, manifestation, and enhancement

jasper: Protection and mental clarity

lapis lazuli: Divine energy, protection, and health

moonstone: Lunar magic, balance, reflection, new beginnings, creative energies, increase intuition, and insight

obsidian: Protection, hex breaker, grounding, and spirit work

tiger's eye: Grounding, creativity, wisdom, insight, emotional balance, and raise vibrations

GLOSSARY

These words are not all used in this book; however, they are included in this glossary to provide a greater understanding of magic.

altar: A table or sacred space that is used for rituals, sacrifices, offerings, or spellwork

amulet: An ornament or charm that is used to give protection against evil danger or disease

anoint: To dress a candle with oils

capnomancy: Seven Nation method of using smoke after the fire has been made for divination

conjure: American folk magic that incorporates African, Native American, Jewish, Catholic, and other Christian and European traditions

consecrate: To make something (typically a tool that will be used for spiritual or magical purposes) sacred

deity: A god, goddess, or divine spirit

divination: The practice of seeking knowledge of the future or the unknown through the use of tools or supernatural means

hex: To cast a spell or bewitch; commonly used for ill will, revenge, or with malicious intent

jinx: Bad luck, caused magically by another person or through breaking a superstition or folk belief

juju: A spiritual belief incorporating objects such as amulets, spells, and talismans to be used in religious practices; derived from West Africa

libanomancy: Divination through the observation of incense smoke; see capnomancy

magic: The ability to subdue or manipulate energies both through natural and supernatural means

novena: From the Latin word meaning "nine," a traditional style of devotional praying in Christianity and Catholicism

omen: A sign or event that is regarded with prophetic significance; can be either good or bad

purification: To cleanse both spiritually and physically

pyromancy: Divination through the use of fire

ritual: A sequence of activities that may involve gestures, actions, or words, performed for spiritual enlightenment, to gain magical momentum, or tradition

scrying: Gazing at various forms and surfaces that offer guidance, prophecy, and answers to potential questions through symbols and images that appear

sigil: Inscribed or painted symbol that has magical power

talisman: An object, inscribed or handmade, that harnesses magical powers and energy

vigil: A time of devotional watching or observance, typically referring to a multiday spell or ritual that may last several hours or more than one day

RESOURCES

SUPPLIES

The Olde World Emporium
@theoldeworldemporium
OldeWorldEmporium.com

This is the shop that I own, with products curated for all magical and spiritual practices, including a large selection of books, crystals, herbs, and altar goods.

Pan's Apothika (AKA Panpipes)
PanPipes.com

This is the first metaphysical shop I ever went to as a child. They carry hundreds of herbs and oils and can custom prepare tools of intention. Vicky, the shop owner and a dear friend, specializes in making individually anointed glass-enclosed candles, typically the seven-day, which is an excellent tool for manifesting one's intentions.

III Crows Crossroads
@3crowscrossroads
Etsy.com/shop/IIICrowsCrossroads

Offering charmed essentials for everyone, this company was started by two of my fellow coven members and blends the magic of traditional witchcraft, voodoo, Santeria, and American folk conjure. Here you'll find soaps, candles, oils, spell kits, and many more enchanting items to get you started on your spiritual journey.

BOOKS

The Element Encyclopedia of Secret Signs and Symbols by Adele Nozedar
This book is a great resource for looking up symbols you may see in wax, dreams, clouds, etc.

The Element Encyclopedia of Witchcraft by Judika Illes
This is a must have for all practitioners, as well as those interested in learning more about witchcraft. Whether you're looking for information on a deity, tool, specific practice, or history, this is the book to have.

The Master Book of Herbalism by Paul Beyerl
This is probably the best book on herbs available for a magical practitioner, offering in-depth information about herb lore, oils, incense, elixirs, and their magical uses.

Voodoo Hoodoo Spellbook by Denise Alvarado
This book is a wonderful resource filled with history, authentic spells, recipes, and more—all focusing on the voodoo of New Orleans.

REFERENCES

Agrippa, Heinrich Cornelius. *Three Books of Occult Philosophy.* Rochester, VT: Inner Traditions, 2021.

Buckland, Raymond. *Buckland's Complete Book of Witchcraft.* Woodbury, MN: Llewellyn Worldwide, LTD, 2002.

Dell, Christopher. *Occult, Witchcraft & Magic: An Illustrated History.* London: Thames & Hudson, 2016.

Editors of Encyclopaedia Britannica. "Trois Frères." *Encyclopaedia Britannica.* October 30, 2015. Accessed May 2022. Britannica.com/place/Trois-Freres.

Huson, Paul. *Mastering Witchcraft.* New York: Putnam, 1970.

Lecouteux, Claude. *Encyclopedia of Norse and Germanic Folklore, Mythology, and Magic.* Rochester, VT: Inner Traditions, 2016.

Leland, Charles Godfrey. *Aradia, or the Gospel of the Witches.* London: David Nutt, 1899.

Luck, George. *Arcana Mundi: Magic and the Occult in the Greek and Roman Worlds: A Collection of Ancient Texts.* Baltimore: The Johns Hopkins University Press, 1985.

Potter, T. W., and Catherine Johns. *Exploring the Roman World: Roman Britain.* Berkeley and Los Angeles: University of California Press, 1992.

Yronwode, Catherine. *The Black Folder: Personal Communications on the Mastery of Hoodoo.* Forestville, CA: Lucky Mojo Curio Company, 2013.

INDEX

A

I

J

K

L

M

N

O

P

R

S

T

W

ACKNOWLEDGMENTS

I'm so grateful and feel so blessed to be able to present this book to you. First, I'd like to thank Ashley Popp and Rockridge Press for giving me the opportunity to create this book. I'd love to thank my parents, Steven and Ingrid, and my grandmother Mom-Cat (aka Lillian), who let me be the wild, imaginative child that I was and didn't try to restrict me or influence me when I became interested in learning more about witchcraft, magic, and the occult. To my brother, whose kindness and genuine support always inspire me. To Vicky Adams of Pan's Apothika (AKA Panpipes), who didn't bat an eye at the intrigued nine-year-old who walked into her shop, and who offered me my first safe haven. To Lana, Leah, and Brenna, who not only took me in as their kin, but also fueled my desires and interests in candle magic. To my crows, Cyndi and Jess, who help me make magic every day. To Nyt Myst, Bloody Mary, Laurie Johnson, and the many other magical mentors and teachers I've had, and, of course, my ancestors and spirits—thank you.

ABOUT THE AUTHOR

For more than two decades, **Mystic Dylan** has studied and perfected his craft in the occult. At the early age of nine, Dylan and his mother frequented a local occult shop in Los Angeles, where his attraction to witchcraft began and grew, paving the way for his career. He mastered palmistry and tarot, honing his skills on friends and family before officially pursuing a formal education in Los Angeles, New York, and New Orleans. His natural connection to mysticism fueled his ongoing study and exploration in the arts of witchcraft, voodoo, conjuration, and shamanism. Now a practicing professional witch, Dylan uses the craft to assist both friends and clients in their personal lives. Born from Cuban, Irish, German, and Native American bloodlines, Dylan attributes his spiritual gifts to his many ancestors who walk and work beside him, guiding him on his sacred journey. He has worked for over a decade as an independent scholar and film and academic consultant. Dylan currently lives and works in Los Angeles, where he runs his brick-and-mortar shop, The Olde World Emporium.

www.ingramcontent.com/pod-product-compliance
Lightning Source LLC
LaVergne TN
LVHW070146120826
845155LV00055B/19

* 9 7 9 8 8 8 6 0 8 6 4 6 1 *